Canton, MA

A
HISTORY
OF
LETTERS

To Laura—
Keep writing those
letters— I'm so
delighted to hear
about what you do—
Phil Yotter
16 March 2021

A
HISTORY
OF
LETTERS

MEMORABLE QUOTES FROM A
MORIBUND ART

Mel B. Yoken

atmosphere press

Published by Atmosphere Press

Cover design by Ronaldo Alves and Avery Hamlin

atmospherepress.com

For Cindy, my muse and inspiration from 1975 to eternity.

PREFACE

In my studies over the years, I've pored over volumes of letters written by such diverse luminaries as Harry Truman, H.L. Mencken, Toulouse-Lautrec, Ernest Hemingway, Dorothy Parker, Robert Frost, Voltaire, E.B. White, George Bernard Shaw, Virginia Woolf, Edith Wharton, Henry James, Theodore Roosevelt, and the indefatigable master of the genre, Madame de Sévigné.

Not all of us manage to live lives of such celebrity or notoriety that our letters are bound and published in volumes appropriate for libraries or gift-giving. But letters are a wonderful solace and even a potent catharsis for anyone.

Ralph Waldo Emerson said that when his writing was blocked, he would write letters to dear friends. John Steinbeck, in writing *East of Eden*, extricated himself from the daily routine of writing books by composing a letter to his editor and close friend, Pascal Covici. These letters were, in Steinbeck's words, "a kind of arguing around for the story," but they also included valuable nuggets of information and fascinating comments and anecdotes for his friend about the events of the moment.

Once upon a time, the only way to communicate from a distance was through the written word. Letters were essential then. And what about history? Most of our knowledge of people and events is based on epistolary communication.

Think about your child's first scribbled note, love letters exchanged with a spouse, sparkling missives we sent to our parents telling how much they meant to us, or a note from a deceased friend. I treasure the insightful, nostalgic letters written to me by longtime friends, former teachers, colleagues, and family members. Over the years, I've kept every one of those missives. Rereading them is like having a good postprandial tête-à-tête with the individual, as they represent a definite connection from one human being to another. They are notations that define a life.

When I began writing to famous and learned individuals in the early '60s, while a graduate student in French literature at Brown University, it was to ask them questions about their work, mainly to help me with my own research. Over the years and decades, I have received sincere, insightful, and sometimes unusual answers from the thousands of people I've corresponded with by post. After all, I could not have delved into the creative mind and perused the brilliant cogitations of poets, novelists, playwrights and others had I telephoned them.

I offer these illuminating, erudite and enlightening quotes from my collection, with the sincere hope that they will amuse, inform, enlighten, and even inspire the reader.

Mel B. Yoken, July 2022

TABLE OF CONTENTS

INTRODUCTION 3

LETTERS:

MUDD, Roger (2), 1928-2021 100
Reporter and news anchor. Dated 8 August 1997 and 8 October 2008.

MURDOCH, Iris (10), 1919-1999 101
British novelist and philosopher. Dated c. 1970, 21 August 1972, 22 May 1981, 5 August 1981, c. 7 August 1989, 2 April 1992, 23 June 1992, c. 6 January 1993, 20 Sept 1993, and c. 8 February 1994.

MURRAY, Albert, 1916-2013 104
Music critic, biographer, novelist. Dated 4 September 1995.

MURRAY, Pauli, 1910-1985 105
Activist, lawyer, poet, author. Dated 6 March 1971.

NIXON, Richard, 1913-1994 106
37th President of the United States. Dated 4 September 1973.

PICON, Molly (5), 1898-1992 107
Actress. Dated 5 June 1970, c. 22 January 1979, 1 October 1984, 19 November 1984, and 14 December 1984.

POIRIER, Richard, 1925-2009 110
Literary critic. Dated 21 November 1988.

PORTER, Katherine Anne (2), 1890-1980 111
Author, journalist. Dated 3 September 1970 and 16 July 1974.

POWELL, Colin, 1937-2021 113
65th United States Secretary of State. Dated 23 May 1991.

POWELL, Richard P., 1908-1999 114
American novelist. Dated 23 October 1992.

RABB, Sidney, 1901-1985 116
Chairman of the Board of The Stop & Shop Companies, Inc., a supermarket chain. Dated 9 September 1971.

RASSIAS, John A., 1925-2015 117
Language professor, Dartmouth College. Dated 6 January 2005.

REAGAN, Ronald, 1911-2004 118
40th US President, 33rd Governor of California. Dated 19 February 1970.

INTRODUCTION

I have known Prof. Mel Yoken for many years as a colleague at the then SMTI (Southern Massachusetts Technological Institute), now University of Massachusetts Dartmouth and, over the past twenty or so years, we have been best friends. In all honesty, I have never seen or been with such a motivated, interesting and talented man, and in so many ways and respects. His knowledge of his field as a Professor of French Language and Literature puts him at the very top of all those in the United States. He has won every award medal and certificate possible, and continues to be a humble, modest—and beloved—individual. Although officially retired from teaching, he is of a most generous mind, always ready and eager to engage with new generations of students. His openness and willingness to share his knowledge are as legendary as his sagacity of the French language, culture and literature. He is, succinctly stated, ambassador par excellence for French culture in the United States, and is greatly admired as such. To wit: Maurice Druon, one of France's greatest writers and former Secrétaire perpétuel of the august Académie française has called Yoken "le porte-parole de la langue française outre-Atlantique." (The spokesperson of the French language across the Atlantic.)

One of Prof. Yoken's greatest accomplishments is his unbelievably vast collection of letters addressed to him over the past fifty or so years. In fact, the collection, housed at The John Hay Library of Brown University in Providence, Rhode Island, has been clearly documented as numbering somewhere around 400,000 letters of truly great import, and this has been often mentioned as one of the most important archives of letters in the United States and beyond. How one man has established such a vast collection is beyond comprehension. What a bonanza for historians and scholars, especially since the art of letter writing is currently moribund and deemed an endangered species.

These letters are written to Prof. Yoken from predominantly the greatest minds in the world. With this in mind, Yoken has started extricating, from many of these remarkable epistles, outstanding snippets which he hopes to publish in book form in the future. I honestly cannot wait to see this book published. In fact, there should be two or three volumes, as there is enough invaluable material for that many.

Prof. Yoken has never rested on his laurels and has always believed in constant perseverance. His determination and acumen are legendary, and I am, therefore, delighted to have written this introduction, and sincerely hope it will be included with the publication of the aforementioned proposed book, a most enterprising idea, indeed.

Prof. Vernon Ingraham, 28 January 2014

"Let your letter be written as accurately as you are able — I mean as to language, grammar, and stops; but as to the matter of it the less trouble you give yourself the better it will be. Letters should be easy and natural, and convey to the persons to whom we send just what we should say if we were with them."

—Philip Dormer Stanhope (Lord Chesterfield)

N.B. Note from Dr. Yoken. Most of the letters in this book were written, often by hand, in a time before the ubiquity of computers and spell checker software. They have been edited for length, readability, consistency and clarity. Beyond these changes, every effort has been made to preserve the intention and spirit of the original correspondences.

AKAKA, Daniel K., 1924-2018

First Native Hawaiian US Senator. Dated 14 March 1991.

. . . who most influenced me to seek a political career, it was Governor John A. Burns, who was in office in the '70s. I served as his state director of the Office of Economic Opportunity, and we had a close personal relationship.

As so often happens in many turning points in our lives, it was not so much my formal relationship with the governor which led me into politics. Rather, it was our chats after work, sitting on the back steps of our then state capitol, our palace when Hawaii was a kingdom, that cast the die. He would often encourage me to aspire to and seek higher leadership positions, not only to help Hawaiians determine their own destiny, but to work in the interests of the greater community. This not only reinforced my inclination and my developing sense of duty to do so, but it also raised my own expectations.

Governor Burns, a transplanted Hawaiian from Montana courtesy of the United States Army, saw many of the inequities which existed in our society in the decade of the 40s, and he felt very strongly that Hawaiians should be a part of the leadership structure and make a difference. Political office, he advised, was one of the best avenues to achieve this end.

In 1976, a congressional seat opened. I ran and won. I have had the privilege of serving in Congress ever since.

Aloha pumehana,
[Daniel K. Akaka]
DANIEL K. AKAKA U.S. Senator

ALBERT, Carl, 1908-2000
Speaker of the House of Representatives.
Dated 9 September 1970.

. . . My visits to Oklahoma average about two a month. When I am in Oklahoma, I attempt to visit various communities in my district. Most often, I schedule specific appearances such as a talk before a civic club, a dedication or ground-breaking for some public facility or a talk before a school assembly. In addition, I try to sandwich in personal visits with consti- tuents who want to talk with me about problems and, when time allows, I set up "office hours" in a particular community to meet with anyone who wants to see me on any problem. When returning to the district, I generally leave Washington Thursday night or Friday morning and return by Sunday night.

It is very difficult for me to name the person who has had the most influence on my career. It has been my good fortune to know and work with a number of outstanding men and women in Congress and the Executive Branch of the Government. One of my predecessors, Representative Charles Carter, had a great influence on my life and career. He came to my school when I was quite young and made a talk about the Congress. It was his appearance which inspired me to want to become a Member of Congress and which directed my efforts in that regard. One of my college professors, Cortez A. M. Ewing, also had a profound effect on my career.

I would consider, I think, my work in connection with education legislation as the most important accomplishment and highlight of my work in Congress to date. Nothing can, of course, surpass the honor given me by the people of the Third District of Oklahoma in allowing me to represent them here. . . .

AMIS, Kingsley, 1922-1995
Author. Dated 8 May 1972.

. . . At present I am about two-thirds of the way through a detective novel, <u>The Riverside Villas Murder</u>, which aims to be a traditional detective puzzle, but will (I hope) provoke some laughs too.

Influences are difficult to spot from the point of view of the man influenced. But let me just say that the comic writers I most enjoy are Evelyn Waugh, Anthony Powell, P.G. Wodehouse and Peter De Vries.

My own favorite among my books is <u>The Anti-Death League</u>, largely, I suppose, because it's the most ambitious so far. . . .

Dated 1 August 1979.

. . . As to poetry, I have written it slowly but steadily over the years and published my collected poems earlier this year. In the UK, that is; I believe they are due in the US in the autumn. I have never written a play for the stage nor am I likely to, since I take no interest in the theatre. I have written five television plays, but outside England they have reached only those countries that buy a lot of British TV, like New Zealand and Hong Kong.

No ideas, I'm afraid, for casting *Riverside*. These days I hardly so much as know by name the new stars. . . .

Dated 8 September 1981.

. . . What I read for pleasure is almost entirely escape fiction – mainly thrillers of various sorts and science fiction. But occasionally, late at night, I read some familiar poetry. As for the present state of humorous writing, it seems to me as appalling as the state of almost everything else. The general level of pieces in the New Yorker and Punch has very much declined. . . .

Dated 14 January 1988.

. . . [THE OLD DEVILS] took me rather longer to write than normal – getting on for two years in all. I revised it more extensively than any of my books since Lord Jim. For your information, the episode involving Billy Moger and Laura went in at the last minute, replacing some only fairly funny stuff about that Welsh-American. And yes, the book has been translated into Finnish and Dutch, and the Swedes have paid me, so I imagine we can count on a translation from them as well. . . .

ANGELOU, Maya, 1928-2014
Poet, civil rights activist. Dated 1 November 1974.

. . . I shall be coming East in February to do some lecture agency arranged appearances, and the best news of all, to receive an honorary degree from Smith College. March 1st I begin rehearsals with a television special which I shall direct. End of March I begin pre-production for the film "I Know Why The Caged Bird Sings," which I shall also direct. With this schedule, I truly can see no time before early June to come East. It distresses me that after having promised to make myself available to you, that now I find my schedule so tight and ungiving, that it's impossible to honor my promises. If at any time the schedule changes and I find it necessary to be East, I shall let you know promptly.

Truly I'm delighted to have the chance to direct television and film . . .

ARMSTRONG, Louis, 1901-1971

Jazz musician. Dated 18 July 1969, written on the back of a diet chart, "Lose Weight, The Satchmo Way!"

. . . My present activities are answering my fan mail, sending out diet charts and pictures. And blowing my horn one hour per day until I return to work. . . . Joe King Oliver cornet player in the good old New Orleans days, and a few others influenced me the most. . . .

ARMSTRONG, Neil A., 1930-2012
Astronaut, first man on the Moon. Dated 15 October 1972.

. . . I do believe that the world in general, and the US in particular, have reaped significant rewards from our space expenditures of the past decade. I would hope that the rate of return would increase over the next decade. The selection of programs to maximize that return is beyond my ability, although I'd be the first to point out that I have my favorites in the race. . . .

ASNER, Ed, 1929-2021
Actor. Dated 8 August 1989.

. . . I'm currently in London filming a mini-series for USA Cable (NOT A PENNY MORE, NOT A PENNY LESS – based on Jeffrey Archer's bestseller) and won't return to LA until November. The British crews work more slowly than I'm used to, but the production is going well and the part is enjoyable. Ed Begley, Jr. is also in the production and the rest are mostly Brits. . . .

Dated 24 March 1993, references his TV series
"Lou Grant."

. . . I was recently in Boston to record a radio play, "Hotel Oubliette," and to do a "Reading Rainbow" for public television. Sadly, I was in and out of town without much of a chance to enjoy the chilly pleasures of New England.

Yes, I do at times miss Lou [Grant], primarily because I think the show and the character were continuing to grow. Of course, the wonderful thing about acting is you never know if a better role is just around the corner.

As for public office... I prefer to act as a goad. My brief stint as SAG [Screen Actors Guild] president was a real eye opener for me, and although I have no love for politicians, I realize the pressures they face. Of course, I am long-winded enough that I could certainly hold up my end if elected! . . .

Dated 2 March 2000.

. . . At the moment I have no project cooking. I'm still doing books on tape.

For some laughs, try Carl Hiassen's latest that I did called "Sick Puppy." I kept breaking up while I did it. Mary [Tyler Moore] and I might meet once a year. . . .

BAKER, Josephine, 1906-1975

Entertainer and activist. Dated 12 May 1974, original French and English translation.

Original:

. . . Comme vous le savez, j'ai adopté douze enfants de différentes nations, religions, et couleurs pour prouver que les hommes peuvent vivre ensemble et on leur donne cette chance. Ces enfants sont grands pour la plupart et ils sont de véritables symboles de la fraternité universelle.

Je suis très heureuse de voir à quel point mon idéal (qui est le vôtre) – car enfin n'est-ce pas que nous sommes tous des frères et soeurs que nous appartenons tous à la même race humaine, cet idéal vous tient à coeur. . . .

Translation:

. . . As you know, I adopted twelve children from different nations, religions, and colors to prove that men can live together if one gives them that opportunity. These children are grown, for the most part, and they are veritable symbols of universal fraternity.

I am very happy to see my ideals match yours – because finally aren't we all brothers and sisters who all belong to the same human race, this ideal is important to you. . . .

BARRETT, William E., 1900-1986
Author. Dated 8 April 1971.

. . . I had a new novel published by Doubleday in March titled
A WOMAN IN THE HOUSE. I did research for that in Munich
and Vienna in 1969. The story is laid in modern Munich, and
it involves a very real problem in Europe; the refugee, or ex-
refugee, who may have adequate papers and may not have. I
am talking now of the Sudeten Germans, the Germans who
were forced out of territory ceded to Poland, the fugitives
from the Iron Curtain Countries. They are interesting people
and present interesting problems. I deal, of course, with only
a few of them and the novel is a love story; but I believe that
the background is authentic and the situations true to the
background. When Doubleday editors read the manuscript of
this book, they commented that I was the first American
novelist to look at modern Europe and present the same
problems that we face in the USA, flavored with the European differences. They urged me to do at least two more
against European backgrounds, and I returned in 1970 for
more research. A French idea suggested to me would move
against the background of Paris, Chartres, Rouen. I made
that triangle conscientiously but could not feel the novel. The
next one, therefore, the one on which I am working, will
again be laid in Germany. . . .

. . . THE LEFT HAND OF GOD is my most successful
book, and no book of mine approached it until THE WINE
AND THE MUSIC came along. That book has done phenom-
enally well. LILIES OF THE FIELD, which many people
consider my most successful book, is running fourth.

My favorite of my books? I believe that I would still say,
as I did many years ago, THE SHADOWS OF THE IMAGES. . . .

[THE EMPTY SHRINE] is laid in French Canada and, as you know, a great many French Canadians cannot, or will not, speak English. I traveled around the Province quite little and had to survive in French, although I speak French badly. Both of these books have been republished in paperback by AVON.
. . .

Dated 1 February 1975.

. . . Books in the offering? Anything to be accomplished in Washington? Ah, yes. The book, which I fondly believe to be my most solid accomplishment, is coming out in April. It is titled LADY OF THE LOTUS and it is the story of Princess Yasodhara, who was the wife of the Buddha. It is a real love story, a solid piece of history. I dug for many, many years to find missing pieces of that story. . . .

Dated 3 December 1975.

. . . My wife and I spent four and one half months in Ireland, with Washington and N.Y. stops on the trip out and the trip back. Our daughter, Marjorie, forwarded most of our mail that seemed important to her, but she shied away from any such heavy items as books. We were rather an elusive target most of the time. We did all of Ireland at our own pace, the North and the South. The North is much more dangerous than newspaper accounts indicate and much more a battle-field. . . .
. . . [LADY OF THE LOTUS] was ignored by the reviewers in the major media, the publications that count heavily, but those who have read the book have liked it. I have a thick sheaf of letters from readers and some wonderful reviews from publications off the main line. Sales will be unimpressive, I fear, but I did not write the book for sales. One happy reward for the book is the fact that I have been invited to be

the keynote speaker at a Buddhist convention – American Buddhists, mostly Japanese – on the first Saturday of March next year. . . .

BEARD, James A., 1903-1985
Chef. Dated 18 June 1973.

. . . The American Cookbook is something I wanted very much to do, and I have been pulling together bits and pieces over the years and have finally put them in a book. We worked on it for five years even though a lot of the recipes and bits of lore had been collected before that. If you enjoy it, it gives me great pleasure, and I am glad it does excite your salivary glands.

. . . I suppose the fact that I was brought up with good food and a great curiosity and that I have been able to travel a great deal all my life and to know various and sundry foods and to know many people who were concerned with them. I don't think any one person has been a guiding light, but it has been curiosity and research. American Cookery has not been translated into a foreign language yet. I do think it is probably one of the three best things I have done. It has given me great satisfaction. . . .

Dated 8 September 1977.

. . . I am very Catholic in my taste about desserts. My great favorite in the pastry world is a Pithiviers with a raspberry puff paste and a delicious almond cream. I love good pound cake and practically any fruit with perhaps a liqueur or wine. Also, fresh raspberries and baked bananas. Sorbets I adore but I'm not an ice cream man. . . .

BERGER, Thomas, 1924-2014

American novelist, author of Little Big Man and Neighbors. Dated 27 January 1995.

. . . As it happens, Neighbors is one of my favorites amongst my own novels, one that was a great joy to write. I never consciously invent a plot or characters: I simply start writing each day and see what happens. With Neighbors I could hardly wait for each new morning to arrive, so I could sit down at my desk and see what was going to happen to Earl Keese. When Ramona first appeared, I was as surprised, and as fascinated, as was Keese himself. . . .

BIDEN Jr., Joseph R., 1942-Present
46th President of the United States, former Vice President, and Senator of Delaware. Dated 13 February 1990.

. . . Beyond all doubt, the person who meant the most to me in the development of my own interest in politics was John F. Kennedy. Kennedy brought his unique combination of energy, enthusiasm, and imagination to the Presidency when I was a senior in high school. The quality of Kennedy's leadership and his vision of America as a still-vibrant land of equal justice and equal opportunity persuaded me that politics is a proud, honorable, and necessary profession in a democracy. It was that conviction that first led me into active political participation, and it remains my strongest political motive today. . . .

Dated 22 February 1991.

. . . Last year's election was, in fact, the most satisfying victory of my political career. You mentioned the percentage of the win, and asked whether it was the biggest margin ever for a Senate candidate in Delaware – I wish I had a straight answer for you. The newspapers all tended to qualify that the margin was "reportedly" the largest ever, and to tell you the truth, I never felt compelled to ask anyone to find out with certainty. I can tell you that the percentage was my largest margin of victory ever, and was very rewarding in that regard. . . .

. . . My recovery from the aneurysm surgery was completely successful, and I'm told I'm actually safer than most folks because my head has been so thoroughly investigated. I have been back to a full and active schedule for more than two years now, enjoying every minute of it – almost.

At such times as illness and war – one very personal and one, as now, very global – the support of family and friends take on a special poignancy. . . .

BOLT, Robert, 1924-1995

English screenwriter, wrote Lawrence of Arabia, Doctor Zhivago, and A Man for All Seasons. Dated 7 March 1975.

. . . I don't know exactly how long it took me to write "A MAN FOR ALL SEASONS." I thought that a play must be possible when I first read Chambers' biography. But it was many years later that I attempted it. However, I suppose I was unconsciously at work on it during that interval. It first took the form of a radio (not television) piece, which was really not much more than a dramatized account of the trial. It was rather stiff but curiously moving and was broadcast more than once. It was while listening to a broadcast of it that I became suddenly convinced that it could be made theatrical. But again there was a long interval before it began to present itself in a series of theatrical strokes. It was when the idea of the Common Man came to me that the thing fell into one piece, and I began writing the play as it now stands. Presumably because it had been gestating for so long, the actual writing, for me, was easy and quick. I think it took me about four months. . . .

BRADBURY, Ray, 1920-2012

American author and screenwriter. Dated Halloween 1974.

. . . I've been writing poetry since Shakespeare ran me over when I was fourteen. But it's taken all these years to percolate and GET GOOD! . . .

Dated 28 July 1975.

. . . Spent the evening with Groucho [Marx] last week – at a friend's house! Groucho sang 8 songs! Great! . . .

BRODER, David S., 1929-2011

American journalist and pundit. Dated 23 December 1981.

. . . it usually takes me about an hour to write a draft of one of my columns and about as long to rewrite it. I like to write in the evening and rewrite the next morning. Obviously, this does not include the time for the reading, interviewing and reporting that goes into the column. There is no way of estimating that, and it varies from column to column. . . .

BROOKS, Cleanth, 1906-1994
Literary critic. Dated 14 May 1970.

. . . I was much influenced by being a student at Vanderbilt at just the time that I was. It was very fine to be under the influence of people like Donald Davidson and John Ransom, and to meet Robert Penn Warren, and to catch the sense that literature was not dead or a mere museum piece, but something very much alive. Later, the Oxford experience and my first introduction to I.A. Richards' work was very important. Later still, I was very fortunate, as I now see, in managing to get a job at LSU where there was the scope and the incentive to strike out and try to devise new critical and teaching methods. There, too, the eight years' intimate association with Robert Penn Warren was crucial. Lastly, it has been very important for me to be here at Yale in the fine department that we have and with theorists of criticism and literature of the caliber of Rene Wellek and William Wimsatt.

I expect to publish later this year a collection of critical essays in New York and London. My New York publisher will be Harcourt, Brace. These twenty-odd essays will indicate the kind of thinking which has been uppermost in my mind during the last ten years.

I am still at work on my second Faulkner volume, though it goes very slowly, what with other activities crowding in on me; and of course I have other works that I hope some day to do.

Most writers are fond of the last work that they've done and I suppose that this is true of me also. I think that my best work is that to be found in my book on Faulkner (published in 1963) and in some of the essays and lectures which will appear in my new collection. But I retain a fondness for *The Well Wrought Urn*. . . .

BURNETT, Carol, 1933-Present
Actress, comedian. Dated 10 December 1971.

. . . I never attended a parochial school, and I have never been treated unkindly by any Catholic nuns. The idea for using the character of the "dancing nun" was based on a personal experience I had when I was a patient at the St. John's Hospital in Santa Monica, which is a Catholic hospital. I was there for the birth of my youngest daughter, Erin, and one day during my recuperation, one of the Sisters on the hospital staff came into my room. After a warm greeting, she began to tell me how much she enjoyed my performances through the years, and, quite enthusiastically, she then told me that she was a tap dancer and had been in show business herself at one time. With that, the Sister gracefully lifted her skirts and proceeded to dance for me. The entire scene was so amusing, and the Sister was perfectly delightful. She had a marvelous sense of humor, and her visit that day has remained with me as a memorable experience. So, you see, there was no malice or blasphemy intended in our sketch. It was done only with love and respect for the many Sisters in the Catholic Church who are so giving of themselves, and who are blessed with a wonderful sense of humor. My three daughters are Catholic, as is my husband, who is the Executive Producer of the show. And, I can assure you, we would never present material that would intentionally offend the religious of any faith. Also, I would like to emphasize that none of our material for sketches is written to express personal comments or views on social, religious, or political matters. We simply try to reflect a humorous side to life . . .

Dated 30 April 1974.

. . . It's almost impossible to do a weekly comedy variety show without offending someone from time to time, when each season involves over one hundred sketches. Taste, of course, is subjective, and therefore an area in which reasonable people may disagree. . . .

Dated 13 February 1975.

. . . I think Garry Moore was more of an influence than anyone, because of his wonderful warmth and the consideration he had for everyone, and the happiness he created among the cast, crew and all those around him. I enjoy appearing in movies as much as doing TV . . . I like the audience, and the [TV] schedule allows me to be with my family more than a movie schedule does. . . .

CARTIER-BRESSON, Henri, 1908-2004

French photographer. Dated 19 March 1974,
original French and English translation.

Original:

. . . J'ai toujours mon appareil de photo avec moi et je m'en sers quand quelque chose me frappe particulièrement.

Je dessine aussi beaucoup. J'ai des dessins qui vont paraître dans le numéro de mai de la revue suisse "DU". . . .

Translation:

. . . I always have my camera with me and use it when something particularly catches my attention.

I also draw a good deal. I have some drawings which are going to appear in the May issue of the Swiss magazine "DU" . . . . .

CHEEVER, John, 1912-1982
Novelist. Dated 16 October 1968.

. . . I finished a novel in August and my present activity is to sit around drinking martinis and waiting for the telephone to ring. I sometimes play soccer with my son. . . . My favorite authors are so numerous their names would fill a telephone directory. . . . I go to Europe once or twice a year. . . I don't think my kind of writer is competent to assess the world situation. . . .

c. September 1972.

. . . I'm very glad you liked [THE WAPSHOT SCANDAL] . . . You might be interested in the circumstances of its completion. When I put down the last sentence I wanted to kill myself. I threw out the sleeping pills and the shotgun shells and scythed a field. I then decided to destroy the manuscript. My wife urged me to get another opinion. I took the book into New York. The compulsion to throw it into an ashcan was powerful. I had my shoes shined and sat through a movie called Hud. I then drank four martinis and walked to the publishers, avoiding ashcans. I gave the manuscript to a receptionist and fled. When the publisher called to compliment me, I thought it the most bitter mockery. I then went to Rome and sulked there until after publication. I was truly miserable. However, I glanced at a copy and it doesn't seem all that bad. . .

Dated 7 February 1976.

. . . Both THE CHRONICLE and THE SCANDAL did very well and have been translated into at least ten languages. There are the Wapshoten, the Wapshotskys and the Wapshotvitch-es. Last year in Boston was not terribly successful because of my health, but since the Cheevers settled in Boston in the 1630s, I can always be counted on to return and give the family bones a shake...

Dated 16 March 1978.

... I'm so glad you like BULLET PARK and you might be interested in its history. I very much enjoyed writing the book, and when it was attacked in *The Times* by a broken-down academic politician named DeMott, I didn't much mind. However, it was remaindered and the paperbacks were dumped into the sea. Two years later, Litvinova did a marvelous Russian translation and the book swept Eastern Europe. A year later it had some success in Japan. It is now doing well in Holland and France and has been re-issued in this country....

CHILD, Julia, 1912-2004
Chef, television personality, author. Dated 9 January 1992.

. . . I enjoyed reading [your] article about learning languages and how very important that has become. Now that America is no longer an island unto itself, we really must go in for languages. Listening to the news about American attempts to do business in Japan without knowing how to speak any Japanese just reinforces our need to learn more. . . .

Dated 30 December 1992.

. . . about fat and dieting, people need to have an adult approach to food – eat the good things: real butter, cream, red meat, etcetera., but they should do so in moderation. We should eat a variety of foods and get exercise in order to maintain our health. . . .

CHRISTIE, Agatha, 1890-1976
English novelist, mystery writer. Dated 26 February 1969.

. . . I am glad you like A MURDER IS ANNOUNCED, but am sorry you like THE MYSTERY OF THE BLUE TRAIN, a book which I have always detested myself for some reason. . . .

. . . [regarding] contemporary writers, my predilections are Grahame Greene, Elizabeth Bowen (quite the tops to my mind), Muriel Spark, a most original and interesting writer, Nevil Shute (though now deceased) as a particularly good story teller. Among American writers of detective fiction, I am a great enthusiast of Elizabeth Daly, The Lockeridges and their Mr. and Mrs. North stories, Craig Rice, whom I have always found enormous fun, and the Nero Wolfe stories – particularly, I must admit, because of the delicious meals described! Of more serious writers, I have enjoyed much of Tennessee Williams, Willa Cather's DEATH OF THE ARCH-BISHOP. I also have always had a great admiration for GONE WITH THE WIND, the only really long chronicle book that I have ever thought an unqualified success, and a success as a film also. Steinbeck's THE MOON IS DOWN and OF MICE AND MEN are two of the short classics. I have not read much of modern French literature, but Claudel's play PARTAGE DE MIDI I shall always remember for the wonderful acting of Edwige Feuillère. . . .

CLINTON, Bill, 1946-Present

42nd President of the United States and Governor of Arkansas. Dated 12 July 1988.

. . . My goals for Arkansas are to prepare our state to deal with the 21st century. To meet that challenge, we must make sure our people are educated and productive and are equipped with the skills necessary to maintain a place in the world. . . .

CRAWFORD, Joan, 1904-1977
Actress. Dated 24 September 1971.

. . . I have done television and film acting recently, and I am also a member of the Board of Directors of Pepsi-Cola Company. I have also recently written a book titled "My Way of Life" with Audrey Davenport, which will be on the stands next month.

So many things have influenced me in my career that I cannot possibly name only one thing.

I believe the favorites of my own films are "Mildred Pierce," "The Story of Esther Costello," "Torch Song," "Dancing Lady," "Humoresque" and the version of "Possessed" that I made with Van Heflin. . . .

CROSBY, Bing, 1903-1977
Singer and actor. Dated 21 May 1970.

. . . Currently, I'm not too active. I do fourteen or fifteen television shows a year – some of them Specials, some of them sports shows, others documentaries, which makes for a fairly active schedule.

I would say that the influences on my career were varied. Mostly what success I've achieved has been the result of good associations, good advice, and good counsel.

And a lot of things that have happened to me have happened through sheer luck.

It would be hard to pick out one person who has been the most influential, because there have been so many.

Future plans for motion pictures are rather vague. The schedule I'm currently maintaining in television comprises quite a bit of work, but more than that, it reaches a great many more people than five or six successful motion pictures could reach.

Also, at my age, it's difficult to cast me in anything in which I would be acceptable. But we still read scripts, look around, listen to suggestions, and something will come on, I'm sure.

At the moment, the only project that is being actively discussed is a comedy with Jackie Gleason, [Bob] Hope and myself, to be filmed in England – but it is not very definite. . . .

CUOMO, Mario, 1932-2015

52nd Governor of New York, father of Andrew Cuomo and Chris Cuomo. Dated 22 February 1988.

. . . I am confident that I made the right decision in not seeking the Presidency. My responsibilities to the people of New York as Governor preclude me from entering the primaries for the Democratic Presidential nomination, and the nominee of our Party should come from the ranks of those who participate in the primary process.

Our Party has a group of capable and experienced individuals seeking nomination for the Presidency. I am confident we will have a nominee with the vision and leadership necessary to carry us to victory in 1988 and govern our nation with distinction in the years ahead.

Whatever else happens, I will continue to do what I can, from here, to see to it that we get the very best leader to steer us through this time's troubled waters. . . .

Dated 10 May 1990.

. . . about my professional baseball career.

I played one season of ball for the Brunswick Pirates, a Pittsburgh Pirates' farm team in Georgia.

I was having a pretty good season until I got hurt trying to make a catch. I continued to play centerfield after the injury, and while it didn't affect my fielding, it did limit my hitting quite a bit.

I was also hospitalized after being beaned. More than thirty-five years later, a reporter who covers the Capitol here in Albany tried to locate the pitcher involved. To his surprise, the reporter discovered that the pitcher lived in the area, and I was able to meet with him and reminisce about our minor league days.

Today, when reporters ask me if I have ruled out a possible course of action as Governor, I usually tell them that I still haven't ruled out playing centerfield for the Yankees. . . .

DAVIS, David Brion, 1927-2019
Historian. Dated 17 June 1971.

. . . The chapters [of THE PROBLEM OF SLAVERY] which have drawn the most attention – the ones on comparative slavery – were precisely the ones I took least seriously. So I supposed that few people had ever ventured into the heart of the book. I'm especially pleased to hear that your brother's high school students have found something of value in the work. They must be very persevering students, and either dedicated or burdened with a taste for punishment. . .

. . . Since 1966, I have been laboring on the sequel volume, but have taken time off to publish three quite different books: ANTEBELLUM REFORM (an anthology, Harper), THE SLAVE POWER CONSPIRACY AND THE PARANOID STYLE (La. State Press); and THE FEAR CON-SPIRACY (an anthology, with a good bit of editorial comment, Cornell U.P.). The sequel, ANTISLAVERY IN THE AGE OF REVOLUTION, is nearing completion in the first draft, but I have no idea when it will be ready for press. Though it covers a much shorter time span (1770 to 1823, roughly), it is in many respects a much more ambitious undertaking. And I find that experience doesn't make writing any easier. I am a slow writer and a slow reader. . . My father, Clyde Brion Davis, wrote twenty odd novels, and while he is virtually forgotten, I would put him high on my list. Aside from this personal note, my favorite novels, and the books that have influenced me the most, are ALL THE KING'S MEN; THE MAGIC MOUNTAIN; MOBY-DICK; HUCK-LEBERRY FINN; THE SOT-WEED FACTOR; THE CHARTER-HOUSE OF PARMA; THE BROTHERS KARAMAZOV; ULYS-SES. I am also a great admirer of Freud, Karl Mannheim, and the late Reinhold Niebuhr. As for historians: Leslie Stephen, Arthur Lovejoy, Ernst Troeltsch, Ernst Cassirer, and Perry Miller – most of whom were not really historians. But then I'm not either, since I majored as an undergraduate in philosophy and literature and took a minimum of history courses even in graduate school. The great thing about getting "out" of school and into teaching and writing is that you can disregard the compartmentalizers. Or almost. . . .

Dated 10 October 1995.

. . . I did, in fact, hold the first Chair in the history of American civilization at the Ecole des Hautes Etudes in Paris in 1980-81. Fortunately, I was teaching only graduate students and could therefore teach in English. While I've done research in French and have read many works in French over the past fifty years, I am usually unable to follow or understand spoken French even though I've had much tutoring. At least since my early twenties, I've had a hearing defect that blocks out most of the higher frequencies. That means I have great trouble with consonants even in English, and have been barred from the joys of even conversational German, though for a time in 1945 I was supposed to be a US Army interpreter. Fortunately, I have one son who is now at graduate school in Princeton who learned French so well when he was seven and eight, living in Paris, that he is now constantly mistaken for a Frenchman even in France. That gives me much joy. . .

DOOLITTLE, J. H., 1896-1993
Military officer. Dated 18 March 1969.

. . . I am presently retired but do some consulting and serve on various boards and committees. Endeavor to keep busy because I am convinced that happiness can be achieved only through service. . .

. . . Three great American presidents have always impressed me. George Washington represented integrity; Abraham Lincoln, humanity and Theodore Roosevelt, patriotism. All exemplified courage. . .

. . . I have never been to Vietnam, know little about it except what I read in the papers. Therefore not being able to shed any light on the subject, I endeavor not to add heat. . .

Dated 29 April 1974.

. . . I am retired but keep busy because it is my firm conviction that happiness comes through continuing service. . .

. . . I thought that both the book and the picture "Thirty Seconds over Tokyo" were very well done. . .

. . . Spencer Tracy made me appear very severe. I'd thought of myself as more fun-loving. . .

. . . The Tokyo Raiders had their thirty-second reunion in the San Francisco Bay Area last week. . .

DUBUFFET, Jean, 1901-1985

French artist and sculptor. Dated 14 July 1981,
original French and English translation.

Original:

. . . Le musée Guggenheim en prendra occasion pour présenter à nouveau, à partir du 31 juillet courant, une exposition de mes travaux. Mais je ne pourrai pas me rendre pour cela à New York. J'en suis empêché par des douleurs vertébrales qui me rendent la marche difficile et m'interdisent de voyager. Elles m'interdisent aussi de travailler debout et de ce fait je dois, pour le moment, limiter mes travaux à des peintures de formats modérés.

Mon procès contre la Régie Renault vient d'être résolu en ma faveur ; un arrêt rendu le 8 juillet par la Cour d'appel de Versailles fait obligation à la Régie d'achever la construction de mon "Salon d'été." Cependant il est incertain que de mon côté maintenant je consente à voir cette oeuvre prendre place en un lieu où elle a été si mal accueillie. . . .

Translation:

. . . The Guggenheim Museum will take the opportunity [of my birthday] to present once again, from the 31st of July, an exposition of my works. But I will not be able to go to New York for that. I am hindered by vertebral pains, which cause my walking to be difficult and which forbid me from traveling. These pains forbid me also from working while standing, and because of this I must, presently, limit my work to moderate-size paintings.

My trial against Renault has just been resolved in my favor; a decree rendered the 8th of July by the Court of

Appeals of Versailles forces Renault to finish the construction of my "Salon d'été." However, it is uncertain that, in my opinion, I would currently consent to see that work take place in a locale where it was so badly received. . . .

EDWARDS, Edwin W., 1927-2021
Governor of Louisiana. Dated 20 February 1992.

. . . I am totally dedicated to being a good governor and will do everything in my power to make the people of this state proud and happy again. I . . . will be pleased to have your advice and counseling from time to time, as I want to do the best job possible. . . .

ELLISON, Ralph, 1913-1994
Novelist and literary critic. Dated 8 December 1975.

. . . INVISIBLE MAN has been translated into fourteen foreign languages. In 1954, during its original publication in France, it was poorly received. With its second translation (1969), it received favorable critical attention, and I enjoyed a moderate sale. Interestingly enough, I was awarded the medal of the Chevalier de l'Ordre des Arts et Lettres in 1968, and this despite the fact that the first translation sold but a handful of copies. . . .

FORMAN, Milos, 1932-2018
Film director. Dated 20 October 1995.

... [Valmont] is a film I am rather proud of in spite of mostly unfavorable reviews and a poor box office, although it is interesting that the film was a huge success in Finland, the only country where Valmont was released prior to Dangerous Liaisons. ...

FRY, Christopher, 1907-2005

English poet and playwright. Dated 8 May 1981,
on writing the play Venus Observed.

. . . To get VENUS written was, in the end, a battle against time. Laurence Olivier had commissioned it to be the opening production of his management at the St. James's Theatre. If you have a copy of RING ROUND THE MOON, my translation of Anouilh's L'INVITATION AU CHATEAU, you will know from Peter Brook's Preface that I interrupted the writing of Venus to do the translation. As a consequence, time was getting perilously close to the opening date at the St. James's Theatre, January 18, 1950. Rather late in 1949, I let Olivier know that I had got to the end of Act II and would be typing it out and sending it to him at once. But by then I was more in the swing of things and working on Act III, and was disinclined to break off to type the second act. I received a parcel from Olivier containing large typewriter ribbon (too big for my Corona portable, vintage 1917), an eraser and a brush to clean the keys: together with a note, which said, "If there's anything else you want, let me know. I'm not making you nervous, am I? I do hope I'm not making you nervous." But this doesn't answer your question about how long it took me to write the play. As you will see, it is hard to say, as the translation also came into that year, and unfortunately, I kept no diary at the time. I only know that I was working long working days, perhaps ten or twelve hours, as the year went into the autumn. I had evidently started work by May 1949, soon after the opening of THE LADY'S NOT FOR BURNING at the Globe Theatre. I had let Olivier have Act I by the 9th [of] June, or at least part of it, to judge from one of his letters. The next reference is on 17th [of] August, by which time I must have got back to it. By Sept. 5th, Olivier is getting a little restless – "If you wouldn't mind, I would enormously appreciate having VENUS finished as soon as possible," he writes. On October 22nd, he writes about "the approaching finish of your play." And his telegram sent when he had received the completed script was sent on November 1st. So it would look as though the writing took about five months.

As you see, your question took me back to the file of Laurence Olivier's letters, to refresh my own memory. . .

GABO, Naum, 1890-1977

Russian sculptor. Dated 4 June 1973.

. . . [your letter is] a satisfaction to any person whose endeavor is to do some work with the wish that others should have it. This is my credo about the raison d'être of a work of art. This should not be understood as a degradation of a work of art, putting it on the same scale as a carpenter's table. Indeed, the carpenter's work is also done for that purpose, for that kind of use. Nothing is a greater prize for the carpenter than to know that the person for whom his work is made is really enjoying it; not only by using it.

So, knowing that, you will understand that I am sincerely glad to hear from you as the representative of the much younger generation. As a matter of fact, my greatest joy is when I get an exhilarated praise of my work from the third generation (my grandchildren). . . .

. . . My endeavor, at the moment, is to fulfill in practice (that means, to build up on a larger scale) a work of mine that was done in the late 20s and meant to be a Fountain. It is now being built in London. As with most of my works, this too was waiting, as there are others still waiting, to be executed on a larger scale than the way I have done them myself. . . .

. . . To be quite truthful with myself, I really cannot say who exactly and what exactly has influenced me. It is correct when I say, Everything in all my life and Everybody with whom I came in contact; artists, scientists and ordinary people, trivial and great events of my time – these are what influenced my work. And to add as a guidance to you in understanding what I say – do not take it as an evasion on my part, since, as you may already know, my basic credo is that everything done by man is a work of art. . . .

. . . I cannot evaluate any of my work out of the chain of the content of all of them. Only in its entirety the work of my life is to be judged – as a whole. . . .

GANDHI, Indira, 1917-1984

First female Prime Minister of India. Dated 6 June 1968.

. . . I was away on a tour of Australia and South-East Asia and was not able to write you earlier.

The relations between the United States and India are good and are marked by a genuine understanding of each other's major problems. It is not merely governmental relations that are good, the relations between the people are even warmer. There are some irritations because the national interest of two countries may not always coincide and because of the dissimilarity of the political and cultural climate. We should not allow the fleeting and the temporary to affect our attitudes.

Regarding Vietnam, obviously there must be genuine desire to end fighting and a better appreciation of the inner strength of nationalism. It is hardly possible to offer snap solutions to such major problems.

French is not as widely studied in India as it ought to be. I am among the small number who learnt it in childhood, but that is because I visited Europe when I was small. . . .

GARROWAY, Dave, 1913-1982
American television personality. Dated 14 July 1975.

. . . April 2 to July 14 has been about the average transmitted time for mail thanks to the crew of delinquent slobs, the very last of whom I shed three days ago when I moved my files and office into my home, and for the first time since 1946, stand free, alone and unencumbered by "help." It's a glorious feeling. About the first thing I am going to do is to answer a letter promptly, and that letter is yours.

I am not the slightest bit ashamed to say that I cried some real tears, and felt some deep satisfaction that *some-one*, and fifteen or twenty years later at that, knew what I was trying to do. I am not complaining, merely reporting that seldom indeed did I hear a word of praise for any *one* of the several elements that I very consciously worked at in every interview – to always listen, for example, did not come easily – Because I had backgrounded myself in other view-points, the temptation to leap in – I had always to remember that the guest was raison d'être for the show and my task, to make him, in his own words, as visible as possible and *then* perhaps, in tempo, to make known other things he had left unsaid, or other points of view. And by God, I think it worked – people, not feeling under attack, loosen before your eyes. And there were many other factors to judge too which were not visible (<u>now</u> I'm really glad I'm writing *you*) to keep him from the ramble, and to not to successfully dodge, and always to keep the time in mind (we were always live, you know, even when taped we never changed a word), so that the whole interview had some shape or form to it when done – oh, a dozen more factors to juggle. But, what a gorgeous job to have for ten years – too good to be true almost. My father, an electrical engineer, urged me repeatedly thru college *not* to specialize, to be a generalist – imagine!

When we went on the air, the critics laughed and roared for a couple of years. But my doubts about the future of the show were summed up unconsciously by leasing a penthouse on Park Ave (the second week I was in town) for four years.

But sadly I had failed to be a generalist, I had become a TV show specialist, "Today" type. I failed to watch the people around me and the business, the lawyers, agents, account- ants, and executives and one day, despite the ratings, the sold-out commercials, the awards, and the critics' praise, I was alone. The NBC news dept. in Nov 1960, took a private survey asking each senator and congressman what newsman they listened to on the TV in the morning. They gave as choices three network men: [Walter] Cronkite, Frank Blair, The ABC man and three local Washington newsmen – six in all to choose from. Seventy-seven percent of the congress said they did listen to TV, and 81% *wrote my name in* on the ballot.

It is Network policy that no individual shall acquire power as in the old radio days – [H.V.] Kaltenborn [Lowell] Thomas etc. – no one with a viewpoint. I was thru at that moment. (I of course did not hear of or see the ballet until 1962).

I was "killed out" of Network TV – that is the phrase used when one of the three networks (they all work together on this) wants someone not simply taken off the air but kept permanently from ever returning in any measure – Pat Weaver, President of NBC (whose creations [gave] NBC great and continuing successes: TODAY, TONIGHT, the "magazine concept" whereby the network controls the program), was so "killed out" in 1955 to make way for Bobby Sarnoff, son of the General, head of RCA which wholly owns NBC – and Weaver has never been able to get a job with any network since.

How do they do it? Power and money. They purchased

my first twenty-two attorneys, for example, they made a "mistake" in their bookkeeping (which, penalty-free, they were permitted to correct) which instituted an IRS audit whose prepared assessment was $1.44 for each dollar I had earned for the three years in question. With interest $1,209,000. Don't laugh. My net worth $300,000.

And on and on. The legal fees to escape from $15,000 excess corporate profits which incurred by investing in a magazine totaled $848,000. I fought . . . as well as [I could] being indignant, innocent and alone (except for two magnificent secretaries) . . . And frankly I am as proud of coming out of New York alive and well to Boston in 1969, as anything I've done. My [TEMPO BOSTON] show was just filler material. My "manager" moved to California and thought I'd give it a fling, no network control of course, but the first two years, lots of local commercials, etc. and then overnight, someone turned off the faucet, and my IRS return for '73 for performance income states it correctly as $23.65, residuals from a rerun of a commercial in S. America. It's hard for me to believe, but I haven't opened my mouth for one dollar for two and a half years! Still fighting it tho – had a major face lift, new teeth, a hair transplant and a new personal manager, and I'm going in for one last fling. Then to the woods!

There, by god. I've actually answered a letter promptly and told a lot of facts that I have never told before – not that they are of the slightest importance. Folks say, why don't you write a book? If I did, I'd have thirty libel suits on my hands at once, and while I have the material to win each one, the cost would be astronomical, and I'm close to broke.

But in good spirits and cheered by your letter spanning all those years. It really does help to make all the trivial worthwhile.

Peace –
Dave Garroway

GELLHORN, Martha, 1908-1998

Author, war correspondent, third wife of Ernest Hemingway. Dated 10 March 1972.

. . . All my books are out of print; they seem to me like some sort of lost Sumerian stone tablets. I never believe anybody read anything or reads anything now. Besides where to find them? As to what I like best – well, I haven't re-read any of them for some time, but I like bits here and there, some stories, and bits of novels. And, for the record and as a record, I think maybe "THE FACE OF WAR," which is some of my war reporting – most of that is lost too – is of value. But really, I don't know. I never was satisfied with any of them the minute they were finished, only had some emotions while doing them. Usually that admirable, desirable sense of sweating: like ditch digging or road building, good hard work. And sometimes a brief sensation of flying, which must be the entire reward.

As to my activities: for two years I've been suffering from writer's block, which is exactly like being lost or stationary in an endless tunnel without light. Everything I started died. Now this last week for the first time I am cross-stitching away at a story, trembling slightly on my unsteady pins, which I believe I can finish. If so, praise the Lord, it might be a real cure and then again might not. I do a lot of things to keep busy, to keep my mind off obsessions, the main one being the abominable Vietnam war. I can't get a visa to go back, and besides have lost my place in the journalism queue; but that war haunts me and makes doing anything, which isn't directly related to ending it, seem futile. I invent jobs – such as being the first female volunteer litter collector in the British Isles. Spent a lovely summer last year cleaning up

Kew Gardens, great fun. I have been spending the winter here where I have a dotty remote house which is nearly impossible to manage, a hermitage on a volcano in the Rift Valley; all brawn, pioneer life. But none of the activities matter much. If I can't write, I don't know who I am. And it is also very hard for me to give writing enough importance in view of the horrors going on in the world: easier to write when the Vietnam war ends, perhaps. . . .

Dated 31 June 1974.

. . . I never thought anyone read me when my books were in print but since all are now (and for a long time) out of print, I feel like an archeological find, if anyone does actually see something I wrote. If you have an archeological type library, which keeps out of print books, I suggest you read "A Stricken Field," about Czecho and "The Wine of Astonishment," a war book I wrote entirely to get Dachau out of my dreams and on to paper. Yes, I wrote about Vietnam in August or September 1966, a series for the Guardian here, called "A New kind of War." It was two years early and got me into the enviable position of being prematurely anti-Vietnam, with the result that I can never get a visa to return. That war haunted me for years and still, and I am ashamed beyond all else of the US government for it. And for the fact that we pay what – over a billion per year? – to keep [Vietnamese President] Thieu rich enough to go on killing.

Yes, various books of mine have been translated but I can't tell you offhand what, and into what languages. And yes, I am trying to write a novel but it moves as smoothly as cement. . . .

GLENN, John, 1921-2016

Astronaut and US Senator from Ohio. Dated 6 February 1984, on the topic of foreign languages in schools.

. . . In today's increasingly interdependent world, it is imperative that Americans communicate better with those from diverse backgrounds. As our trade becomes more and more international, our businesses need more people fluent in language. But it would be more shortsighted to encourage foreign language study merely for economic reasons. By learning a new language, Americans open up rich new vistas to comprehend the world about them.

Many students, frankly, are frightened by the prospect of learning a foreign language. But with patient, dedicated, knowledgeable teachers, they can overcome this understandable reluctance and master this new skill, which will mean so much for their personal development. The results easily justify the investment of time and effort, especially now when the very future of our planet depends on effective communication among people with different histories, cultures, religions, and political and economic systems. . . .

Dated 24 August 1988, on the topic of returning to space (he would indeed return ten years later).

. . . I'm ready to go into space again, any time – provided that I would be making a contribution to our space program or our knowledge of space. However, I suspect that at the present time, senior citizens are not going to be high on the list for astronaut duty and feel that perhaps my best contributions now will be made as a US Senator.

I very much appreciate your support, and hope that I

may be in Massachusetts sometime this fall. I will be campaigning for the Dukakis-Bentsen ticket, but I do not yet know all the places I will visit. . . .

GOLDBERG, Rube, 1883-1970

American cartoonist and inventor. Dated 29 July 1969.

. . . It is difficult to name the men who have influenced my career. One, of course, was my father, who guided me over my formative years and later supervised my contracts when I was too timid to put the right financial value on my newspaper cartoons.

I was also influenced in my early style by Tad Dorgan and Eugene Zimmerman, whose style of humor and penmanship I admired very much.

I added a new room to my place here and am now making an oil painting to hang on its wall. The style is broad and comic. . . .

GOLDEN, Harry, 1902-1981
Writer and journalist. Dated 15 August 1969.

. . . At present, I am preparing to go to Israel to write a book, ONLY IN ISRAEL for Putnam's, due next year.
The men who have helped influence me in my life have been my father and Carl Sandburg. . .

Dated 28 August 1970.

. . . I use my leisure time to write books. I have three coming out next year; THE GREATEST JEWISH CITY IN THE WORLD, THE BINTEL BRIEF, AND THE ISRAELIS.

I ran the Carolina Israelite for twenty-six uninterrupted years and I had enough of it.

I come to the Boston area often, at least three or four times a year. . . .

GORDIMER, Nadine, 1923-2014

South African writer, Nobel Prize in Literature recipient.
Dated 18 March 1971.

. . . I have just finished revising and polishing seventeen stories written over the past five years, and they will be published either this Fall or the Spring of '72 as a collection under the title, LIVINGSTONE'S COMPANIONS. At the moment I am writing the commentary for a small documentary film; my first effort of that kind. After that – well, I don't know; GUEST OF HONOUR was my work and life for nearly four years, and one must have time to fill up anew. In October, I shall spend a semester at Columbia University as one of the visiting writers with whom graduate writing students may discuss their problems.

Many writers have influenced me, I suppose; some of them are writers who no longer interest me, but no doubt their influence remains. When I was very young, D.H. Lawrence, Henry James, Hemingway, Woolf, Proust, much later, Camus (I like to think of *THE LATE BOURGEOIS WORLD* as something I could not have written without Camus). *A GUEST OF HONOUR* is, I suppose, my baggy monster of a novel (as James would have said), but to me it is the one that owes least to any influence. I like best *having written it*, above all my books; but this is not to say it is my best... about that I don't know. It is a private achievement because it is something that I always wanted to do: to break out of the mould of my kind of subject and writing, and write a political novel in terms as personal, as dramatic and non-didactic as the most 'delicate' of my short stories. I think that *LATE BOURGEOIS WORLD* is my best-written novel; *OCCASION FOR LOVING* satisfies me; *WORLD OF STRANGERS* – definitely not. . . .

Dated 28 October 1975.

. . . I much appreciate your understanding of my novel *[THE LATE BOURGEOIS WORLD]*. You are right in detecting the influence of Camus, and what a fruitful one, too! I feel that from the point of THE LATE BOURGEOIS WORLD, I learnt how to combine a strong narrative with the nuances on which my writing had depended too heavily until then. It is still one of my novels with which I am the least dissatisfied. It went into a number of translations (in fact, the Swedish one is just about to be re-issued) but was, and remains, banned in my home country... Jonathan Cape, my British publishers, are about to re-publish it in a uniform edition of my work which will begin to appear over the next few years. It did not sell too well in the United States and has only just gone out of print on the original edition.

I did not ever know a real Max, but he was a prototype of the period, and the kind of action he took, the kind of trial in which he was involved, was based on real happenings. . . .

GROPIUS, Walter, 1883-1969
Architect. Dated 15 November 1963.

. . . I am still active in my firm, The Architects Collaborative, building myself, particularly in Germany and recently in Buenos Aires. . . .

. . . I have just published a book APOLLO IN THE DEMOCRACY, McGraw-Hill, New York. . . .

HARDIN, Clifford M., 1915-2010
Secretary of Agriculture, Chancellor of the University of Nebraska, Vice Chairman of Ralston Purina Company. Dated 9 March 1973.

. . . [regarding] why I left Government when I did, and the answer to that is quite simple. Having opted for the most interesting assignments, we had neglected to provide sufficiently for retirement years. I therefore needed another career following Government service. At age fifty-six, you realize that you are reaching the age when such opportunities will begin to diminish. The situation here at Ralston Purina is unusually interesting and challenging and [fits] precisely with my personal needs and interests. The President was aware of my concerns beginning with the day he invited me to join his administration and was extremely cooperative in helping me make the transition.

I did leave the Cabinet with reluctance because I enjoyed working with the President and felt strongly that we had succeeded in turning the agricultural economy around. The events in the past twelve months have proved the validity of that view.

While I have several responsibilities at Ralston Purina, one of the most interesting is that of supervising our Research and Development activities in attempting to search out new areas for corporate expansion.

The number one agricultural problem for many years has been that of insufficient returns for capital and labor invested. It has been my view for thirty years that this situation could be substantially corrected if American farmers could get freer access to world markets. The first step in that involved reshaping the farm program so that domestic support prices and other restrictions did not have the effect of denying access. This was accomplished, and exports have been expanded from about $6 billion per year to in excess of $10 billion. Both production and net farm income have been expanded. I have oversimplified, but I have at least touched on what I consider the most significant area of concern.

Two or three impressions might be of interest to you as a scholar. I was surprised and pleased at the unusually high quality and high competence of some of the senior civil servants in Government. I was also surprised at the large number of able people who had important assignments and who were willing to drop what they were doing to join us in Government.

I am grateful for the opportunity that I had to work with a great President. I am also grateful for the wonderfully stimulating experience of spending more than thirty years in the university community. . . .

HATCH, Orrin, 1934-2022
American Senator. Dated 7 February 1989.

. . . I would say that it is my parents who have probably had the most influence on my political career. They taught me the value of hard work and the privilege it is to be an American. I also admired President Franklin D. Roosevelt's unwavering courage in the face of great personal and national challenges; and, more recently, President Reagan has been an inspiring example of sound leadership. . . .

Dated 26 March 1991.

. . . The resistance of [Lithuania, Estonia, and Latvia] against Moscow's repression demonstrates the strong desires shared by these peoples for democratic self-determination, which I consider to be a natural right of all people. . . .
    . . . Too often in debate about US policy towards Lithuania, Estonia, and Latvia, the issue has been framed as a choice between granting full diplomatic recognition to democratic governments or do nothing. This is a completely false dilemma. Rather, the United States should undertake diplomatic steps short of full recognition that would advance Baltic independence and increase in Moscow's calculation the international political cost of coercive policies. . . .

Dated 30 May 2001.

. . . about my appearance in the movie "Traffic." I am pleased with the final result of the movie. While I do not support the gratuitous violence and excessive language, I generally agree with its message of creating greater and more effective interest in our problems.

Stephen Soderbergh's film is a stark portrayal of the multi-faceted drug war. I guarantee that any teenager who is playing with the notion of doing drugs will think twice about it after they see this movie. In this respect, I am proud to be associated with such a well-crafted movie. . . .

HIGGINS, George V., 1939-1999
Author, lawyer, professor. Dated 31 May 1983.

. . . The only response that I can deliver honestly . . . about translations of [COGAN'S TRADE] is that I know it was published in the United Kingdom. I have been renewing Swedish, Norwegian, Danish and Dutch contracts on THE DIGGER'S GAME, which preceded COGAN by a year, so if it was translated into those languages, I will know next year. The Italians seemed to lose interest in my writing after DIGGER, and the Germans never say much of anything after they have bought one or two, so I can't be certain about them. As for the Turks, while they did buy one set of rights from me, they generally just go ahead and take what they want without asking. Same for Spain.

You may be interested in A CHOICE OF ENEMIES, which Knopf has scheduled for publication in January. Ballantine has the rights to THE PATRIOT GAME, which came out last year, but when they expect to use them, I don't know. I enclose THE RAT to tide you over until then. . . .

HIMES, Chester, 1909-1984

Writer. Dated 1 December 1970.

. . . At the present time I am engaged primarily, along with my wife, in making minor improvements for the sake of comfort in the house and studio we have recently built here in the province of Alicante in Spain and planting a garden, which, in view [of] this barren, stony terrain, is a major project. I am doing very little writing at the present, but I hope in the near future to concentrate on writing the second volume of my autobiography, the first volume of which is to be published by Doubleday & Company in September 1971, under the title of THE QUALITY OF HURT. . . .

. . . What has influenced me most in my career is my desire to give word to what I think is the knowledge of humanity, which has accumulated in my intellect from a repressed, and at times, hectic life. . . .

. . . My favorite book [of mine] is a little-known novel published as an original paperback by NAL in 1955, entitled THE PRIMITIVE, because my protagonist in THE PRIMITIVE, Jesse Jackson, a black writer, beaten to his knees by the circumstances of life, saves himself from total defeat by killing his white mistress and achieving immortality. . . .

HOLMES, John Clellon, 1926-1988

Author and poet. Dated 12 November 1970.

. . . It's becoming more and more rare for a writer, in this image-dominated age, to receive any sort of personal response from his readers . . . writing is a lonely task performed over a long period of time (with an equally long period of time between the completion of a project and the moment when it reaches the world) . . .

. . . At the moment, I am trying to finish two books, and I'm feeling like a man who, while riding a mare, plans to break a stallion – perhaps tomorrow. The first, which is nearly completed, is an account of a trip to Europe three years ago – part memoir, part Lawrencian travel piece – to be called WALKING AWAY FROM THE WAR. It lacks about seventy pages, and parts of it have appeared (or will) in *Playboy, Holiday, Venture* and other magazines. The second project is a novel set in L.A. this year against the background of Tate-Manson, the new wave of occultism and sexual "freedom," and the generally black state of the Republic. I'm having my problems with it because – well, if I could tell you why, I wouldn't be having them, I suppose. . . .

. . . I started as a poet, and feel closest to Blake, Whitman, Lawrence, Yeats, Pound, Williams, Roethke – all those who speak urgently, directly, and verge on a mystical cast of thought. While writing GO, I was up to my eyeballs in the Russians, particularly Dostoyevsky, who taught me how to dramatize a scene from the inside, how to create a certain density of milieu, how to catch the frenetic mental climate of youth. During this time, I was much influenced, as a man and as a writer, by Jack Kerouac (some acknowledgment of my debt to him is suggested in a collection of essays,

NOTHING MORE TO DECLARE – Dutton, 1967). THE HORN betrays Jack's influence in its overall mood, but I was reading Faulkner and Melville during that time, and I know that I profited from Melville's contagious reach of language. I was trying to hint at a myth (the artist as American), and the rhetoric seemed one way to snag it. Still, my most abiding interest in fiction is character, and I was much affected by Shakespeare and Balzac in THE HORN as I was by Melville. By the time of GET HOME FREE, I was drawing away from language-as-an-end, and getting closer to the sort of deep saturation in character and milieu (as being inextricably related) that I was rediscovering in Lawrence. GET HOME FREE was written in an attempt to liberate myself from a longish period of creative aridity, and thus its compass was kept small. The private aesthetic aim of the book might be said to be an attempt to catch the random nature of con- temporary reality. The book was improvised in some ways (the two major sections were written first, the three N.Y. sections last), and though I think of it as a minor work, I'm fond of it, remembering the fears of talents-wasted that I overcame in the writing of it.

All in all, I suppose that, for me, the most maddeningly, stubbornly, consistently creative writer in English in this century is Lawrence. I think that he was attempting to describe a new sort of consciousness (that was only begin- ning to emerge in his time, but has become almost universal in ours), and I think he bears the same relationship to this age, the same sort of prophetic relationship, that Dosto- yevsky bore to his. The works or each only became compre- hensible after thirty years or so.

Among other writers that I continue to read and from whom I always learn: Balzac, Dickens, Tolstoy, James, Proust. Of more recent vintage: Fitzgerald, Genet, Brecht, Mailer, Frisch. And continuing through all: the Russians – Chekhov,

Gorki, Turgenev, even Sholokhov.

What I miss in the contemporary novel is richness of character, a wide-ranging curiosity about life, that neutrality of the novelist which used to be the clearest sign of his reverence for life, and the sad good humor about follies and flaws which is now replaced with bitterness, cynicism and rage. I compare the secret fondness of life that even a misanthrope like Celine exhibited as against the ugliness and life-hatred of so many writers today, and can see no real comparison.

I, too, have taught in universities on occasion – seminars in modern literature and creative writing workshops. I've energy, inquisitiveness, talent and knowledge, but also found a sense of alienation from what I can only call "the impulse to civilization" that is disheartening. But then the "barbarians" of the past – the Lawrences, etc. – were also thought to be battering down the gates, and it's only now that we can see how terribly hard they were trying to warn us, and what efforts they made to reconnect us with an older, a more essential continuity. So I try to confine my worries to my workroom, and be patient. . . .

Dated 26 October 1975.

. . . I haven't looked at [THE HORN] for years, but I still get an occasional letter from people who have – though God knows where they find copies. The book, along with most of my others, has been out of print for years.

I agree . . . about electronics having taken a serious bite out of attention to print by young people, though, of course, my students, trying to be writers, read a lot more than their peers. Still, even they spend a lot of their time with the tube, or seeing movies.

My books have been translated into Danish, Swedish,

German, Italian and a little French. They've all been published in England, and my first novel, GO, is being reissued here in the States sometime next fall by a small publisher who is putting out a series of "first novels that were neglected."

WALKING AWAY is still searching a publisher. So far, most of them have given it rave notices but feel that people are sick of the war (though the book actually deals with a trip to Europe, it is rife with reflections about Vietnam and America), so perhaps it'll have to go to a small house, or a university press. I am currently at work on a novel (well, I'll be back to it when we return to Old Saybrook around the first of the year), and there are a few other projects on the fire as well.

There's been no book since NOTHING MORE, except WALKING, but I've published poems and interviews and articles in the last years. The novel may take me another year or more to complete. . . .

HOWARD, Maureen, 1930-2022
Novelist. Dated 25 March 1993.

. . . I've been digging out from under and teaching. I don't see Margaret Flood [in EXPENSIVE HABITS] as autobiographical unless all characters are projections of one's very own language – that view. . . .

. . . I've not been much translated. Language, that again, seems to hold back the foreign publishers. They like a simple American, which I guess I don't write. So be it. . .

Dated 26 April 2003.

. . . I am in the midst of the new book, which takes place, in part, in Connecticut and Rhode Island, but the mother of the family, during a restless season of her life, takes the children on excursions. One is to New Bedford, to the Melville Chapel, or so I call it, the chapel which I have visited. You will know it, no doubt, the wonderful place described in *MOBY-DICK* with the pulpit like the prow of a ship and so forth. I recall there were plaques on the wall, just as the Master reports, but of course many were more recent – the thirties and forties, some almost contemporary. My scene is set in 1943, wartime. Do you think there is someone in New Bedford at a Historical Society who might answer my question? Also, I have the chapel opened by a custodian, thinking that during the war, many places were not open that lay along the shore.

But it is only fiction, so I suppose I can make [it] up. What I'm after in this strange visit is the mother's attempt to read some Melville to the children, a failed performance. I'd be most appreciative if you could come up with someone who knows the answers, and there might even be a pamphlet that gives the names of some of the Portuguese fishermen that went down to sea... how that's worded. I forget if those plaques said fishing boat or whaler. . . .

JONES, Robert Tyre, 1902-1971
*Golfer, founded Augusta National Golf Club and
co-founded the Masters Tournament. Dated 7 May 1970.*

. . . For over twenty years, I have been suffering from a progressive disease which now has me almost completely disabled. . . .

. . . My present activities are absolutely minimal, and I make it a point never to name the greatest golfer of this or any other period. . . .

KENNEDY, Edward M., 1932-2009

US Senator from Massachusetts. Dated 7 March 1994, about his mother, Rose Kennedy.

. . . My mother has had many blessings throughout her long and abundant life, but the blessings she cherishes above all are the loving concern of her many devoted friends throughout the country and the world.

She is still a dynamic spirit in the Kennedy family household, but is, of course, quite frail at 103 years of age. She enjoys the visits of her grandchildren and is still very interested in my work in the Senate. I try to visit her almost every weekend at our home in Hyannisport.

Mother's great inner strength comes from two sources. The first is, of course, her deep and abiding faith, which has sustained her in times of grief and doubled her joys. The second is the warmth and compassion of her family and friends whose love constantly reminds her that her life has made a difference for us all. . . .

LaCAMERA, Anthony, 1914-1984
TV columnist. Dated 4 June 1979.

. . . Since I saw you, I've been doing other speaking engage-ments and, thank goodness, they're still turning up. Along with the not-too-frequent "Good Day" appearances, they keep me "involved" – not to mention "solvent."

The "Good Day" association is a little frustrating, I must admit, because the appearances are too far apart and not long enough. . . .

LANG, Fritz, 1890-1976

Filmmaker and screenwriter. Dated 10 May 1974.

. . . When you start your last decade or you are living already in it, you begin to think if the work you have done has reached the special audience for which it was made: the youth of our country.

Unfortunately, my eyesight is diminishing rapidly. I can't work anymore and when I go over my work of more than fifty years, I would like to know if I have achieved what I went to do.

I was honored by many awards and decorations, but the real and positive proof to my question is a letter like your kind letter of April 30, 1974 . . .

. . . My activities of today are – as I can't film anymore as I explained in paragraph two of this letter – lectures in colleges and universities.

It is correct that I appeared as an actor in the film "CONTEMPT" by Jean-Luc Goddard. I played myself. Otherwise I never played a part in my own films.

It is very hard to say which are my favorite films. From German Films probably "DESTINY" and "M." From the American films maybe "FURY," "WOMAN IN THE WINDOW," "SCARLET STREET" – (it is hard to say) – and definitely my only French film, which I shot for the French 20th Century Fox: "LILIOM". . . .

LEA, Tom, 1907-2001.
Artist. Dated 17 June 1970.

. . . I am in the middle of writing another novel, yet untitled, about some Mexicans in the State of Chihuahua in the years 1918-1919; I hope to have the writing done by the end of 1971 and see it published in 1972. Meanwhile, my production as a painter continues about as it has during the years since World War II – half the time painting, half the time writing. . . . my best and favorite work is always the one I am working on. When it's finished, my best and my favorite is the work I intend to do next. . . .

Dated 11 January 1989.

. . . I've been painting, not writing, for the past several years. There's a piece of a novel getting colder and colder here on the backburner; I doubt if it ever heats up to start cooking again. In the meantime, I'm pursuing the profession and the adventure for which I was trained, trying to be a better painter. . . .

Dated 4 February 1991.

. . . I regret to tell you that the half-finished novel you mentioned is still half-finished. I've been painting rather than writing for a long time now, and it's hard to say when I'll turn from linen canvas to yellow copy paper again. . . .

LEWIS, John, 1940-2020

Representative for Georgia, civil rights leader. Dated 23 July 1998.

. . . about the people and events which have influenced me, one of the greatest, and earliest, influences on my life was the Reverend Martin Luther King, Jr. I was just fifteen years old when I first heard the voice of Dr. King on the radio, as he preached a sermon called "Paul's Letter to the American Christians." I heard that sermon at a time in my life when I was beginning to question some of the injustices I witnessed growing up in rural Alabama, where I lived on my family's small farm. My father was a tenant farmer – a sharecropper. I attended segregated schools and was refused entrance to a public library because of the color of my skin. I saw the signs everywhere that divided our world into "white" and "colored." I will never forget hearing that sermon. For me, it was an inspiring call to become more involved in the lives of others, and to treat every human being with a sense of fairness, justice and compassion. It was an answer to some of the questions I had begun asking and provided a way of dealing with the problems of our society. It really seemed to point out, for me and countless others, a way up and a way out.

A few years later, when I was attending the American Baptist Theological Seminary, I sent a letter to Dr. King, telling him that I wanted to be the first African American to attend Troy State College in Troy, Alabama. Dr. King wrote me back and sent me a bus ticket to travel to meet him in Montgomery, Alabama. There, I met Dr. King for the first time. It was the beginning of a long relationship that lasted many years, and throughout many pivotal moments of the

Civil Rights Movement.

Thank you for enclosing your article, "My languages, myselves." I could not agree with you more about the importance of multilingualism, in this country and around the world. I believe we are a nation of immigrants. We should celebrate the wealth of knowledge and experience that a variety of heritages brings. Learning more than one language helps us to do so. . . .

LORD, Walter, 1917-2002
Author, historian. Dated December 1981.

. . . Winston Churchill once said Britain and America were two great nations separated by a common language. I think of that whenever I find Tommies wearing singlets instead of undershirts, driving lorries instead of trucks, and embarking in rowing boats instead of rowboats. Three phrases, however, are the same in both countries: Thank you; Merry Christmas; and Happy New Year! . . .

LYONS, Eugene, 1898-1985
Journalist and writer. Dated 9 March 1976.

. . . The primaries circus bores me no end. It's a dog-fight for a job, not a clash of ideas or visions. In the whole lot there is not one who measures up to the stature of President of a great country; not one in whom I could take pride as spokesman and symbol of America. Not even Reagan, though I like him as a person. His general "ideology," in so far as he has it, is closest to my own, but intellectually he is no match for the great Presidents of our past. And the others are even worse. My overall feeling is that our country – and the West at large – have suffered a tragic decline in leadership. Democracy in practice, alas, has produced mediocrity and moral sterility.

Your Massachusetts primary, most analysts claim, showed a trend to the right, the distance being marked by Scoop Jackson as against McGovern in 1972. I hope the claim is right. Certainly it is opened to question by the Hiss story leading off the campus paper of the SMU [Southeastern Massachusetts University]. The level of juvenile intelligence the article discloses is shockingly low. It's bad enough to invite Hiss, worse to regurgitate all the pro-Hiss and anti-Chambers bilge. It's not "a slice of history" that came to the university but a package of stale myths. It happens that I sat through the trial at which Hiss was found guilty. No honest jury could have brought any other verdict. It was not a question of who was to be believed, as between Hiss and his accuser – although on that level, too, Hiss showed himself less credible. His guilt was proved to the hilt by physical evidence.

But how are college youngsters to know or understand?

They absorb their judgments from politically prejudiced media and, presumably, from teachers reared by and dedicated to a Liberal Establishment. Oh well . . .

MARCUS, Jacob R., 1896-1995
Rabbi, scholar of Jewish history. Dated 6 March 1980.

. . . I wish I had time to read the many lovely things that my friends send me. If I did, I would be able to do no work here of a scientific nature. Every social science field is so vast that one cannot even hope to keep up with his own specialty. What a tragedy.

You ask me about intermarriage. We Jews who have been reared Orthodox are not inclined to perform intermarriages, but if we do not we will lose at least 25% of our young folk who marry out. If we perform intermarriages, we have a chance to keep them within the fold. . . .

Dated 3 July 1980.

. . . I have tried vacations and they make me physically ill. I find it impossible to relax except through work, which I enjoy. My best vacation is to lock the doors and to sit at my desk, to forget the world about me and to immerse myself in the papers in front of me. . . .

Dated 19 September 1980.

. . . Jews do respect tradition. Religion, on the whole, is always a conserving influence. We tend to hold on to practices that are apparently outdated.

In politics, we Jews here and in other lands tend to be on the liberal side. We want change because change protects us and helps us. We are very eager for equal treatment. We have suffered too long. We do not ask for affirmative action; we want no favors. We want everything that is accorded others. We work hard and expect others to work equally hard. We have come up the hard way, and we are of the opinion that others can rise as we have risen if they evidence intelligence, effort and integrity.

I think we are unusual in the sense that we have strong ethnic feelings. It is my opinion that there are few peoples in the world who are ethnically close as are the Jews. It is possible that I am wrong in this assumption. . . .

Dated 14 September 1984.

. . . I do not speak any French. I have no ear for languages. My problem is complicated also by the fact that I am almost deaf.

I was with the Army in France for almost a year. That was in 1918-19. I went to Paris to study in 1925 and was married there. I left, however, after a few weeks to be with my bride in Berlin. I think I have not been in France since 1925, but I cannot recall.

I do very little traveling now. I have had many invitations to lecture and I have cut them down radically; I am eager to stay home and finish my big book on American Jewry. . . .

Dated 28 March 1988.

. . . I am always glad to hear from friends. I have been telling friends that I read Hebrew, and I read from right to left and accordingly, I am now 29 and holding.

There is no question in my mind that computers will be part of the future. I have one but I have never touched it, and it's all Chinese to me. My secretary has one and she is struggling with it, but she is getting able to handle it; she still has problems. Of course, computers are in their infancy. They will do magnificent things in the generations yet to come. I agree with you that foreign languages are important. A foreign language widens the horizon of every person and separates him from the people who have no linguistic skills.

I did not realize that there were so many people of Portuguese descent in your town [New Bedford, Massachusetts]. I think it would be wise to encourage the teaching of Portuguese in the public school system. This will integrate the family; that would be a contribution to Americanism in the finest sense of the term.

I read with interest what you tell me about your Japanese students. The amazing thing is that although there are no Jews in Japan – practically none – anti-Semitic literature is appearing in the country. It is also true that Japan wants nothing to do with Israel. I cannot understand this unless Japan, apprehensive, realizes that the Israelis are potential rivals even though they are a small and inconsequential. . . .

Dated 29 September 1989.

. . . You speak of the secret of my survival. My mother lived to be over one hundred. Why do I work so hard? I have no choice, I am a workaholic. If I can't work, I get sick. . . .

Dated 20 November 1989.

. . . There is no question that the Christian holiday is a real problem for observant Jews. I instruct my students who are to become rabbis what to do with respect to the Christmas holiday problem. I tell them in June to go and see the superintendent of schools and ask him to eliminate Christmas celebrations from the public school system because we believe in separation of church and state. I do not advise them to go in December right before the holidays. Christians are very sensitive to this issue right before Christmas. It would be wrong to broach the subject at the eleventh hour. . . .

Dated 15 April 1991.

. . . The College gave me a ninety-fifth birthday party. They didn't make it altogether clear that I was going to have a celebration, but I guessed at it and when I was called in I was fully prepared to rise up for the rebuttal.

I also told the people that next year I will not be ninety-six but ninety-five; after that I will be ninety-four. I explained to them that the reason I was going backward is that there is no future in going forward. . . .

MARX, Arthur, 1921-2011
Author, son of Groucho Marx. Dated 5 July 1993.

. . . [It] usually takes about a year for me to research and write a book, give or take a few months on either end. The book I just finished, THE SECRET LIFE OF BOB HOPE, which will be out sometime this fall, took a little over a year. I would have preferred more time, so I could check out a few more facts, but I was under a deadline, so I finished in just a year.

I enjoy writing biographies the best, if I know the subject well, and I don't get a lot of problems from the people I need to interview to get some of the facts. I take that back, I enjoy biography writing, but I prefer to do fiction, as I am getting sick of doing research.

I like doing plays, but, alas, it is so hard to get a play on these days because of the enormous production costs that you have to wait too long before you can see them on the stage. My partner and I started on GROUCHO: A LIFE IN REVUE in 1980, and we didn't get it to off-Broadway until 1986.

I really enjoyed doing my first mystery, but I'm not sure that the critics did, although I did get a good review in the *Chicago Sun-Times*, and a number of my friends liked it. . . .

. . . I know I received one funny rejection from our play THE IMPOSSIBLE YEARS when my partner and I first wrote it. One of the biggest literary agents in New York wrote us that our play would never "go on Broadway." Well, it went longer than he did. It played 656 performances and I'm still getting royalties from it. . . .

McGILL, William J., 1922-1997

Psychologist, President of Columbia University. Dated 14 March 1984.

. . . When I retired from Columbia in June 1980 (ten years in that post during these difficult times was enough), my wife and I moved back to our home in La Jolla. She had kept it during the years we lived in [an] old house, and it was still waiting for us when I stepped down. As you know, La Jolla is as close to paradise as you can get in this world. I have office space on the University of California campus in La Jolla.. . . what I have been doing:

1) I wrote a book on the student unrest of the '60s titled THE YEAR OF THE MONKEY (McGraw-Hill, 1982).

2) Joined the board of Occidental Petroleum in Los Angeles in 1981, and remained on the board of Mc-Graw-Hill.

3) Became a trustee and board chairman of United World College (really a prep school) of the American West in Montezuma, New Mexico (1982).

4) Became a trustee of the Weingart Foundation (1983, Los Angeles), the Lounsberry Foundation (1980, New York City), and the Western Behavioral Sciences Institute (1984, La Jolla).

5) Got back into the technical areas of my old discipline – detection theory (psychology and electrical engineering). I am writing a book in this area starting next fall.

6) Drafted and started to write a book on Columbia (still writing).

As to my achievements at Columbia, the most important, in my opinion, were:

1) Reaching out successfully to disaffected students and restoring reason to its rightful place in Columbia College.

2) Returning the College of Physicians and Surgeons to its traditional position near the top of American medicine (with a great deal of help from Dr. Paul Marks and his distinguished faculty)

3) Persuading the Trustees (beginning in 1973) to borrow nearly $80 million at extremely favorable rates (circa 5%) from the New York State Dormitory Authority, although at the time the University was heavily burdened with five years of accumulated indebtedness. We then invested this new borrowing at rates in excess of 15% and used it to undertake the restoration and reconstruction of the entire campus. The swing in interest rates made the new construction virtually self-financing. Mike Sovern, my successor, has continued the program with even more success. It has transformed Columbia totally. . . .

MICHENER, James A., 1907-1997

American author. Dated 1 November 1968.

. . . My present activities are primarily political for this year. I have been secretary to a great convention that succeeded in rewriting our [state] constitution when all the surrounding states had failed.

The authors I have particularly liked have been men like Balzac, Samuel Butler, Thackery, Tolstoy, and some little-known ones like Goncharov, Multatuli, Couperus.

I was not satisfied with the movie version of HAWAII but I was not ashamed of it. It was a good honest effort, it was a picture that conveyed a great deal of historical fact, and my disappointment stemmed only from the necessity that producers faced of cutting parts out of the book and leaving the most important members lying on the ground. I hope that at some future time they may go back to it. . . .

Mel B. Yoken

MOERS, Ellen, 1928-1978
Academic and scholar. Dated 24 October 1973.

. . . How do I rank [Mme de] Stael? As everyone else does, I
guess: as one of the major formative minds in the history of
European romanticism and probably, for what little it's
worth, still the front-ranking woman in the history of ideas.
I'm rereading her DE L'ALLEMAGNE and similar works, but
don't expect to find anything worth comment there in terms
of "women's lit." as a viable critical subject. The work I must
include is her CORINNE because of its enormous influence
on English and American women up to the end, almost, of
the 19th century. And as with Sand, it's not easy to tell why.
My thoughts on the matter will appear in a chapter of my
book on THE HEROINE, which I've promised to the Harvard
English Studies for pub. in Spring 1975; I'm starting work on
it next month.

   As for SAND – my God no, not Elle et Lui, but the
massive and marvelous HISTOIRE DE MA VIE is her great
autobiographical work. As to the novels, yes I warmly share
your pleasure in FADETTE and the other DE L'ALLEMAGNE
(on which I wrote a few words, re George Eliot, in an article
in the *Fall 72 Columbia Forum*, that might interest you.) But
the problem is that they delight in large part because of the
wonderful prose, lost in translation – and most of the
Eng/Amer Sand readers read her in trans. and were bowled
over by the big, bourgeois-to-upper-class marriage books,
such as INDIANA and CONSUELO. It's one of those that I
prayed to fall in love with. Please – if you go on reading GS
and fall for one of the non-peasant books, please let me know
at once to spur me on; there are so many. I just labored
through a pretty dreary one called ANTONIA (in English)

98

which, as you might expect, Willa Cather liked.

No time for 20th c. women – question I'm often asked and often think about. Plath I'll bet on now as permanently major; many of the young women writing now (Gilliat, Frame, even Roiphe) seem to me potentially important if they go on to major works. I leave out obvious current "big names" because most are not my cup of tea. But reading voraciously – everyone anyone talks to me about with enthusiasm. So do please write your own tastes, French or otherwise. . . .

MUDD, Roger, 1928-2021
Reporter and news anchor. Dated 8 August 1997.

. . . I am not a linguist, though I am married to a woman who is fluent in Italian and French with a rough grasp of Yugo-slavian. Alas, not much has rubbed off. . . .

Dated 8 October 2008.
. . . I am in good health with major assistance from Tylenol and Bourbon . . . After leaving PBS in '92, I taught at Princeton and my alma mater, Washington and Lee, a seminar on politics and the press. . . . I am not still teaching. . . . For ten years, I hosted documentaries on the History Channel until retiring in '04 . . . This spring, Public Affairs published my memoir "THE PLACE TO BE: WASHINGTON, CBS AND THE GLORY DAYS OF TELEVISION NEWS." . . . I met Eudora [Welty] some years ago, became immediate friends, saving a bed for her when she came to Washington and when she died went on the Welty Foundation Board to help raise money to preserve her home in Jackson, MS as a gathering place for Welty scholars. . . .

MURDOCH, Iris, 1919-1999
British novelist and philosopher. Dated c. 1970.

. . . I have no favorites among the books, except that I am always most interested in the ones that I am writing. When they are finished they are good as far as I am concerned.

I have been influenced by many writers – Homer, Plato and Shakespeare (I hope) – and Beckett and Henry James and Raymond Queneau (I believe). . . .

Dated 21 August 1972.

. . . I have no special feelings about any of the books except the one I am actually writing. They recede very fast. This one [THE RED AND THE GREEN] took me, I think, about eighteen months to write. I don't know about sales. This book combines a lot of my Irish childhood memories. . . .

Dated 22 May 1981, regarding a character in her book NUNS AND SOLDIERS.

. . . No, Gertrude was not a portrait of anyone I know. I don't model characters on real people. I am working on a novel at present, and also trying to write some philosophy. . . .

Dated 5 August 1981, regarding what kinds of fiction she likes.

. . . I have no special favorite, except that I like the later ones better. . . . I read and reread the good – 19th Century novels, but not much modern (contemporary) fiction. (Not much after J. C. Powys.) . . .

Dated c. 7 August 1989.

. . . Yes, I write every day (except when forcibly prevented)!
. . .

Dated 2 April 1992.

. . . I am recovering from that unusual episode, but still feel
rather tired and (most unusual) averse to eating! However, I
am getting better and better. I don't think [A FAIRLY HON-
ORABLE DEFEAT] is my best – I think the later ones are
better still – but I'm so glad you like it! . . .

*Dated 23 June 1992, regarding traveling and the episode of
illness mentioned previously.*

. . . Actually, I am still rather tired (though recovered) and
want to avoid long journeys at present. . . .

Dated c. 6 January 1993.

. . . surely foreign languages should be taught in elementary
school. A language acquired at eight (as I did French) can
stay with one's whole life – and so on – oh it is so important
– so mind-enlarging, happy-making, useful, etc. etc., what
joy. Alas, over here there is a slight decline. I had Latin and
Greek (as well as French and some German) at my enlightened boarding school. I have become the school "visitor" and,
visiting, discovered that Greek is out, and Latin is not
compulsory. They have also abolished cricket, a game which I
played ardently at my prep school and boarding school.
(Rounders instead – contemptible!) . . .

Dated 20 Sept 1993.

. . . I don't, except for one or two remote occasions, read
translations of my books. It may be rather risky. One Italian

translation included a footnote explaining that ALICE IN WONDERLAND as an opera by Gilbert & Sullivan – also, UNDER THE NET was translated <u>Dans le filet</u>, not <u>Sous le Filet</u>, losing the sense of the title. (Later, as I asked, they changed it!) . . .

Dated c. 8 February 1994, regarding a French review of the French translation of <u>Nuns and Soldiers</u>.

. . . No, Gallimard hadn't alerted me about LES SOLDATS ET LES NONNES! They are about to translate LE CHEVALIER VERT, I am told from other sources. They never communicate with me!

Yes, I met J. P. Sartre v. briefly in Brussels* shortly after the war ended. We talked for about half hour. He was very kind to me, treating me properly as le maître to student. (I gathered he had never heard of Wittgenstein.) I liked him very much and later wrote about him. Also, in Brussels, an enlightened bookshop keeper thrust into my hand a book I had not . . . been able to find earlier: L'ÊTRE ET LE NÉANT. At that time I had scarcely heard of SEIN UND ZEIT, to which L'ÊTRE ET LE N[ÉANT] owed so much. No, I didn't meet Simone de Beauvoir, but had her pointed out to me in a restaurant by Raymond Queneau! (I later wrote to her but received no reply.) . . .

. . . *in fact, about three days after the war ended – I was then in UNRRA [United Nations Relief and Rehabilitation Administration] en route for the Displaced Persons camps in Austria. . . .

MURRAY, Albert, 1916-2013
Music critic, biographer, novelist.
Dated 4 September 1995.

. . . My writing workload is such that a phone chat is easier for me than a note, even one as brief as this one. . .

MURRAY, Pauli, 1910-1985

Activist, lawyer, poet, author. Dated 6 March 1971.

. . . [DARK TESTAMENT] has not been widely reviewed but appears to get around by word of mouth. I had to learn some years ago that once a book is published, it is on its own and the author must not fret about its fate: Thus, letters . . . which come every once in a while are pleasant surprises.

DARK TESTAMENT is the only book of poems I have published; it represents a selection from the many poems or fragments of poems I wrote during the 1930s and 1940s, which seemed to me representative of my thinking and feeling. Since that time, I have been so preoccupied with the law in relation to civil rights, women's rights, etc., that I've had little energy or inclination toward sustained effort at poetry. Poetry, it seems to me, represents a strong tide of emotion that cannot be sufficiently expressed in any other medium. It is not exactly compatible with law review articles which have taken up much of my writing time during the past two decades. I must also confess that I have not kept up with contemporary poets except in a desultory fashion. I seem to be stuck with an earlier tradition – T.S. Eliot, Lola Ridge, Stephen V. Benet, Paul Engle, Frost, Sandburg, Countee Cullen, Gwendolyn Brooks. I particularly like Margaret Walker's "For My People" and some of Bob Hayden's work, but must confess that I have to work at LeRoi Jones.

My present activities have been restricted for health reasons and upon the advice of my physician, so I am trying to avoid too many extra curricula involvements. Therefore I do not contemplate any lectures in the Boston area in the immediate future. I do hope to get a little writing done during the coming summer, if possible. . . .

NIXON, Richard, 1913-1994
37th President of the United States.
Dated 4 September 1973.

. . . faith in our country continues to be strong, and that the people of the Nation – who have contributed so much to the progress of mankind – will help this Administration to achieve the great goals we seek for America and for the world. . . .

PICON, Molly, 1898-1992
Actress. Dated 5 June 1970.

. . . At present I am preparing to leave for London and Yugoslavia to do the role of Yente The Matchmaker in the film version of Fiddler On The Roof – this will keep me busy from July 4th to 1971!

After that ? ? ?

My one real Svengali in my work has always been Yonkel (my husband of fifty years . . .)

And my favorite role still remains Yonkele – which Yonkel wrote for me fifty years ago as my first starring vehicle!

We are both fine – looking forward to a new adventure and hoping not to let you down in all our future undertakings – . . .

Postmarked 22 Jan 1979, written on a playbill for the revue "Those Were the Days."

. . . This is my current play – which we tried out in Phila[delphia] – and will resume in October – on tour and then New York – It's in English Yiddish and reaches both Jews and non-Jews – and we hope will have the fantastic success it had in Philadelphia and reach you both – . . .

Dated 1 Oct 1984, begins with reference to included form with biographical information.

. . . I think from the printed letter on t'other side you will have a fairly good idea where and how I've spent my eighty-six years – until now, when unfortunately I was stricken by Bell's Palsy and for almost two years have been unable to do my "act."

I am beginning to be able, I hope, to continue my performances and have already written a new "act" – which I call "MAMA LUSHEN," because I want to get to the young people who understand so little Yiddish –

So – if and when – I feel able to go back to "work," I'm sure you'll hear about it – . . .

Dated 19 November 1984.

. . . I am eighty-six years old – going on eighty-seven – and have performed all over the world – from age six to eighty-four – and now . . . out of nowhere Bell's Palsy attacked me, and for almost two years, I have been unable to perform . . .

I would have to do my "act" to New Bedford audiences – and as soon as I will be able to – I assure you – I'll be doing my best to accept your offer to appear for your audience – . . .

Dated 14 December 1984.

. . . How I wish I could write and say – I'm ready to "act" again – But I'm still under doctor's care fighting Bell's Palsy – about which mama would have said, "You shouldn't know from it!

I shall be eighty-seven on my next birthday and I'm afraid to take on any "job" although I try to make myself believe I'll be able to do it – so – all I can advise you to do – is call me again and hopefully I'll be able to accept your offer – and don't worry about Honorariums – I have a feeling I'll work for anything just to be on the stage again –

Once when I was married to my Yonkel, I was supposed to do a concert in Miami on my birthday, but somehow Yonkel couldn't be there too – so he sent me a wire –

For the girl who grows Older every year And Younger every day! –

So – here's hoping I'll be "younger" and able to be with you and your meshpoche. Meanwhile, pray for me – for good health – good news and above everything shalom (peace) . . .

POIRIER, Richard, 1925-2009
Literary critic. Dated 21 November 1988.

. . . what counts most are those like yourself who read the books, care about the writers they discuss, and go to the trouble of letting me know about it. Nice to think of you and your family in New Bedford. When I'm not editing this magazine in New Jersey, I live in New York City and sometimes miss my own hometown of Gloucester, Massachusetts . . . .

PORTER, Katherine Anne, 1890-1980
Author, journalist. Dated 3 September 1970.

. . . My present activities are, as usual, trying to get my writing done, in spite of the confusions and interruptions and demands of daily existence – less usual, a year of recovery from a series – three – of major accidents, months in hospital and nursing home – in plaster casts; months at home in bed or a wheelchair –

I have four books in progress, if it can be called that – of my published works, I have no favorite – They are finished and gone – I loved writing them, and I love what I can write now. And I hope you will like them too if ever even I am allowed to finish any of them. . . .

Dated 16 July 1974.

. . . It is distressing to me to be so late answering your letter, which had such a lovely idea for a Katherine Anne Porter Day to be held in late November of this year.

It is a most tempting prospect, and I wish I might say, "Of course, I will come," but I cannot make any engagements, especially one as far away as this, because I am in a rather precarious state of health. There is not much encouragement from my present condition to think that I might be able to travel at all during the next several months . . . If there is any occasion in this world that I look forward to with joy and delight when it occurs is a festival of this kind. I do have, you are right, a pleasant number of invitations to attend parties, to speak, to review books . . . and I never tire of them. I have always made superhuman efforts to attend every one.

There could be a little hope that I might be able to attend in November, but I dare not make a promise. If you could give me a deadline, as editors do, for my latest possible answer, I could live in hope and still not delay your program. Can you let me know about this? I should be happy to hear from you.

I have been in the throes of writing about the moonshot cruise in December, and it would be only an article for – don't be shocked – PLAYBOY. If you are surprised to find me in such company, so was I. But it was really an exciting sort of thing, which I am very glad to have seen. I don't know when it will be finished.

With my deep thanks for your lovely invitation and an assurance that it would delight me to accept it, I am

Sincerely yours,
Katherine Anne Porter

POWELL, Colin, 1937-2021

65th United States Secretary of State. Dated 23 May 1991.

. . . Many people deserve credit for the success of Operation DESERT STORM. I am especially proud of our brave Americans in uniform who showed such courage, sacrifice, and skill during the operation. These fine troops deserve our respect and gratitude. . . .

POWELL, Richard P., 1908-1999

American novelist. Dated 23 October 1992,
written in smallcaps.

. . . I APOLOGIZE FOR THE FAINT TYPING OF MY
TYPEWRITER. IT IS AN OLD PORTABLE OLYMPIA, AND I
CAN'T SEEM TO REPLACE IT. YEARS AGO I BOUGHT AN
ELECTRIC TYPEWRITER AND HATED IT. I'M SURE I
WOULD HATE A COMPUTER THAT TYPES EVEN MORE. . . .
. . . "I TAKE THIS LAND" WAS IN LINE FOR FILMING
FIVE OR SIX YEARS AGO. COUNTRY MUSIC AND TV STAR
MEL TILLIS BOUGHT AN OPTION ON THE FILM RIGHTS,
AND KEPT RENEWING THE OPTION FOR TWO AND A
HALF YEARS. HE HAD A SCRIPT WRITTEN IN HOLLY-
WOOD AND ANOTHER IN NEW YORK CITY, SO HE SPENT
QUITE A BIT OF MONEY ON THE PROJECT. I UNDER-
STOOD THAT HE PLANNED TO MAKE A SIX-PART
MINISERIES FOR TELEVISION. HE DROPPED THE PRO-
JECT, HOWEVER, AND MY AGENT WAS NEVER ABLE TO
GET AN ANSWER FROM THE TILLIS OFFICE AS TO WHAT
HAPPENED. MY GUESS IS THAT HE MAY HAVE DIS-
COVERED THAT THE PLANNED MINI-SERIES MIGHT COST
UPWARDS OF TWENTY MILLION DOLLARS, AND HE
COULDN'T RAISE THAT AMOUNT. I WAS REALLY SORRY
THAT HE DROPPED THE IDEA. MY SORROW WASN'T ON
ACCOUNT OF THE MONEY I LOST FROM NOT GETTING A
COMPLETE SALE, BUT BECAUSE I WANTED MEL TILLIS TO
MAKE THE FILM. HE IS A SOUTHWEST FLORIDIAN, BORN
IN TAMPA AND RAISED JUST SOUTH OF LAKE OKEECHO-
BEE, AND SO I WAS SURE HE WOULD DO A FINE JOB ON A
MOVIE ABOUT THE AREA WHERE HE GREW UP. . . .
. . . MY REACTION TO THE PRESIDENTIAL DEBATES. I

FEEL A BIT GUILTY ABOUT ADMITTING THIS, BUT I AVOIDED LISTENING TO THE DEBATES. MY WIFE WATCHED THE DEBATES, AND I CAUGHT GLIMPSES OF THE PERFORMERS, BUT I COULDN'T FORCE MYSELF TO WATCH. SHAME ON ME. . . .

RABB, Sidney, 1901-1985
Chairman of the Board of The Stop & Shop Companies, Inc.,
a supermarket chain. Dated 9 September 1971.

. . . I suppose that my original inspiration came from my own parents and my good fortune in having had some excellent basic Hebrew education. Also, I have always felt that my tutorial instructor at Harvard, who was Professor Harold Laski, had a good deal of influence in emphasizing the need for social responsibility. The background of our family has always been to participate in community activities and with that sort of environment, I think one naturally gravitates towards accepting his responsibilities. . .

RASSIAS, John A., 1925-2015
*Language professor, Dartmouth College. Dated 6 January
2005, written in jest.*

. . . The order from Mesopotamia containing all the relics that
you and I unearthed on our expedition has just arrived. I
examined them immediately and [found] them to be in great
shape, except for the one of King Totouchem. I thought it
would be appropriate for us to donate the King to a University of distinction, but on the other hand, we ought perhaps
to hold a bazaar and go to the highest bidder.

Please let me know what you think.

> Sincerely,
> John A. Rassias

P.S. In the event I will be on my yacht cruising the Aegean,
please send your letter to my office in Pakistan. You will, I
am sure, recall the address. . . .

REAGAN, Ronald, 1911-2004
40th US President, 33rd Governor of California.
Dated 19 February 1970.

. . . [regarding] who has influenced me the most – writers, actors, statesmen and so forth. My problem is that the list could grow so long. I can remember back to radio days and a wonderful gentleman named Peter McArthur, physically handicapped, but the kind of man who heard the troubles of others and usually was able to send the teller of troubles away better off.

Later in the picture business, the number is great. Strangely enough, actors who are supposed to be so temperamental and jealous of each other are the most helpful to beginners and to their fellow actors. They are always ready to give helpful hints, advice with regard to taking direction, parts, and so forth. Pat O'Brien, at a particular moment in my life, was responsible for what became a great forward step.

Now in this new life I wouldn't know exactly where all the input has come from by way of reading advice and counsel from statesmen, men in government, and men who had been in government. However, I find my mind turning to one name above all others, and one I never had the pleasure of meeting. I'm speaking of Winston Churchill. Few figures in history have been such a magnificent example of the right man in the right place with the right answers when so many needed him. . . .

. . . [regarding] the most important problem facing our nation and our state, we must find an answer to the welfare situation, which virtually has us in the position of ancient Rome, when the mob, supported by the state, had become a viable political force. Financially, welfare and its associated programs are increasing in cost several times as fast as the increase in our revenues. But of even greater importance is the human problem involved. Somehow, this gigantic hodgepodge of overlapping programs has led to a purely materialistic philosophy of thinking that by filling a person's belly with bacon and beans, we have solved his problem forever. The truth is that these programs, while meeting the responsibility of providing food and shelter, are destroying the character and the spirit of the people we should be helping. I believe it is absolutely essential to have a welfare program whose goal is to work itself out of existence, whether it can ever be achieved or not. Welfare, like a doctor, should be operating on the basis of healing the patient, so the patient no longer needs his services. It is fashionable today to say that our economic problems in government spending are all brought on by the military. The military is a nickel and dime operation compared to the wastefulness of our social reform programs. . . .

RIDGWAY, General M. B., 1895-1993
US Army General. Dated 10 May 1974.

. . . About seven years ago, when I had passed my seventy-second birthday, I decided to cease making formal addresses, and I have ever since adhered to that decision, excepting only my appearances at the War Colleges of the Armed Forces. I had a two-day session on two successive years at the nearby Naval War College, when my dear friend, the late Vice Admiral Richard G. Colbert, was President. Those and similar sessions at the Army War College I found immensely satisfying and stimulating because of the exceptionally talented Faculty and Student personnel present.

Presently, and for years past, I have been very fully engaged in the field of national security problems, working with groups in the private, not governmental, sector, such as The Brookings Institution, the Carnegie Endowment for International Peace, the National Strategic Information Center, etc. It is absorbing, and with a heavy correspondence – without the benefit of secretarial or stenographic help – with plenty of outdoor work around our home, I am fully occupied. . .

. . . It would be hard for me to choose [the high points in some of my last active duty posts], but I think you would find them described in my two books, if by chance they are in your Library: "SOLDIER," Harper & Brothers (now Harper & Row), 1956, and "THE KOREAN WAR," Doubleday & Co., 1967. . .

Dated 17 November 1979.

. . . I have no solution for the problem of the hostages in our Iran Embassy. There are too many factors, none of which are known outside the top levels of our Government. What I do think our Government should recognize at once is that we draw ever closer to involvement in a major war, and then having recognized the stark reality of that grim fact, should begin without delay to correct the present grave deficiencies in our military posture. The greater our readiness for war, the more we are likely to avoid it, the greater deterrence. In any case it is what others may do in areas of our vital national interests, which can cause war to erupt with relatively little warning in various parts of the world.

I continue to work intensively on major problems of national defense, notably on SALT II [Strategic Arms Limitation Talks] and our lamentable unpreparedness for a conventional war of major proportions. The arguments against SALT II are clear and convincing to any objective analyst. The state of our unpreparedness is being increasingly revealed to the public, despite the Administration's refusal to divulge it, as it was so clearly shown in the Mobilization and Readiness Test conducted at top levels a year ago last October. . .

Dated 13 November 1983.

. . . "I believe today's overriding imperative is to explore every avenue, to exhaust every conceivable means and method to bring the governments of the USSR and the US into solemn and irrevocable agreement to ensure that a nuclear confrontation does not take place."

As nearly as I can now recall, those words were spoken by me at one of the numerous meetings of individuals of national stature, deeply concerned over ways to avoid major armed conflicts in the 1980s. That meeting was chaired by the then President of Yale University, Dr. Kingman Brewster.

Whatever decisions may flow from such a premise, now or in the years ahead, must be reached with full realization that unilateral disarmament, a nuclear freeze at current levels of weapons in possession of the two superpowers, must be categorically rejected by the US.

The leadership of the USSR is an implacable and deadly enemy, seeing us as the only major obstacle to the attainment of its long-proclaimed objective, world hegemony.

In this world of brutality and savagery, our Nation is the champion of human dignity and freedom. If we were to fail in that role, the light of freedom would be extinguished, perhaps for millennia.

It will not happen. We shall keep that flame burning whatever the cost, I feel sure. . .

Dated 5 August 1986.

. . . I do not recall the NEW YORK TIMES article of mine on "Disengaging from VIETNAM," but do remember an earlier one in LOOK Magazine and a much more detailed later one in FOREIGN AFFAIRS, though I have forgotten the date and my personal papers and official records are in the US Army Military History Institute, Carlisle Barracks, Pa. 17013.

I am blessed with good health, but most of all with a noble wonderful wife, and with as much correspondence and involvement in national defense projects as I can handle. I would be quite unhappy if I did not have pretty full days.

The nationally known writer and historian, Clay Blair, brought out a book last year: RIDGWAY'S PARATROOPERS. It is a splendid portrayal of the operations of US Airborne (Parachute as well as Glider) in Europe in WWII, and particularly of the personal relations between senior US airborne Commanders and between them and their counterparts in both US and British units. The publisher is Doubleday & Company, N.Y. Blair is co-author of the autobiography of General of the Army [Omar] Bradley, published some two or three years earlier. . .

RYAN, Cornelius, 1920-1974
Irish-American journalist and author. Dated 15 June 1971.

. . . Regarding the mail, I find myself today somewhat of a cross between a psychiatrist, a marriage bureau and a lost and found department! I get letters from veterans all over the world with whom I have contacted over some twenty-five years regarding the war. I suppose that I am the only international veteran's administration in history!

I live quietly here with my wife, who is a novelist and our two children. I suppose I should be more ambitious and become more academically involved, but honestly, I find that there just isn't enough time to do everything. I am still a Research Fellow at the University of Manchester but I have no ties with any American universities – though I suppose I should become involved.

Currently I am working on the third volume of my war series called, "A BRIDGE TOO FAR," which deals with the greatest airborne drop of World War II on a series of bridges between the Belgian border and Arnhem on the Lower Rhine in Holland. Had this imaginative and daring plan succeeded, there is no doubt in my mind that the war would have ended in November 1944. I think that the work which has been underway now for some six years may prove to be a modest companion to "THE LONGEST DAY" and "THE LAST BATTLE." Actually, although it has been written as the third book, it is, in fact, the second volume for it picks up where "THE LONGEST DAY" left off, i.e. from Normandy to the halt of the Allied advance in September 1944. . . .

. . . I write some historical papers, lecture occasionally and it seems that every time a film producer decides to do a picture on World War II, he winds up on my doorstep. I have little time for that sort of enterprise, for my experience with Hollywood has been that they drain you of historic truth and subvert it to their own purposes. I did, however, write the screenplay for "THE LONGEST DAY" (20th Century) and "THE LAST BATTLE" (MGM). Whether "THE LAST BATTLE" picture will ever be made is debatable. Very reluctantly, I was persuaded to write the screenplay for a very bad book by Leon Uris called, "ARMAGEDDON." Never have I dealt with such a mishmash. Completing that, I returned to my studies again and doubt very much whether that picture will be made either. Frankly, when this book is finished, I don't know whether I shall continue on with World War II. I'm not so sure whether I have much more to say about it at least in the narrative form which I am accused of having developed.

I am flattered by the fact that you consider my production as "literary." I cannot agree with you. I don't really consider myself anything more than a fairly good and accurate journeyman writer, and believe me, I remain overwhelmed by the success of my books. Speaking very frankly but honestly, I must say to you that it is a terrible responsibility to be the largest selling nonfiction American author in the world. It is absolutely frightening to me. You cannot make a single mistake anymore, etc. You cannot socialize to the point of enjoyment without something outrageous appearing about you somewhere. My wife and I, according to the columns, have been divorced at least a dozen times (we have been happily married for twenty-one years) and my children, aged fifteen and eighteen, have had the devil's own time in their schools – all because their father happened to write books called "THE LONGEST DAY" and "THE LAST BATTLE." Everybody considers that you are not only a millionaire but a multi-millionaire, so hardly a day passes by without some extraordinary demand on your time. They all forgot the terrible capital outlay involved in producing these books. Anyway, that's another story altogether.

You ask about the film "THE LONGEST DAY." In view of the above paragraph, I should begin by saying that Mr. Darryl Zanuck, who produced the picture for 20th Century Fox, recently announced that it grossed $54 million and that 20th Century made a profit of $35 million. It may come as a surprise to you to learn that I only received $135,000. So, I cannot exactly claim to be a great booster of the film! Technically I think it was excellent. Had the entire book been translated onto film it would have run for twenty-four hours. The fact that we were able to get 60% of the book compressed into three hours was some achievement. I lost two full years of my life in the making of that film, and that I regret more than anything else. As war films go, and remembering that Zanuck himself, even after I had finished the script and returned to the US, added some ghastly lines (he fancies himself as a writer) – even in spite of all this, I still think it is in its own way a kind of classic.

I suppose what bothers me the most is that the five books I wrote preceding "THE LONGEST DAY" have long since been forgotten. I suppose they were bad books anyway. What I will do after this third volume, I don't really know. Although I am an American, I have been toying for some time with the idea of returning to Trinity, possibly in some dull occupation as a Master, which would avail me the chance to read a la John Hersey did at Yale. Possibly, all of that is an unattainable dream! My son will be finished high school next year and I suppose he will want to go to an American college – if he can get in! My daughter a couple of years from now. It's all as simple as that . . . in my opinion, "THE LAST BATTLE" is a much more mature book than "THE LONGEST DAY." I consider the latter more of an evocation than a history whereas "THE LAST BATTLE," which curiously sold much more than the first volume, is less recognized. . . .

. . . [regarding] who influenced my career. I wish I could

come out with some brilliant answer. I'm afraid I can't. Stendahl, Forster (I think "A Passage to India" is still one of the finest novels in the English language), Proust and the like had a lot to do with my interest in writing. Really though, I am quite ignorant about much in the field of literature. It always amuses me to hear people loudly exclaim over Joyce, Faulkner, etc.

I, for example, have never been able to get through "FINNEGAN'S WAKE" and Faulkner has always left me cold. I spent a long time with Hemingway in World War II. We shared a jeep together for many months, and I suppose some of his discipline rubbed off on me. I once asked him about his convoluted sentences. He told me that he had received an education that was almost nil but that he had learned Spanish at a very young age. As he wrote, he found himself thinking in Spanish and then translating into English. This was his only explanation. With me, writing has to have a kind of rhythm and emotion. Sometimes it is almost orgiastic. I have to put myself in the place of the characters I am writing about. Always my great problem is that I am totally restricted by accuracy. I cannot deviate from precisely what occurred nor dare I add. I presume that my reader will understand what I am trying to say to him without my batting him over the head. I try to take the reader with me through every moment of the story, for if I have recon-structed the event correctly and I can get him to experience everything that occurred, I know then that he will have the theme and the message without my having to slug him with a dull analysis. Does that make sense? I am not sure, but it's the best I can do. . . .

SACHAR, A. L., 1899-1993

Historian, founding president of Brandeis University. Dated 7 June 1979.

> **N.B. Note from Dr. Yoken.** *David is our second son, and he did apply for admission to Brandeis and graduated from the University in 2001.*

. . . [Regarding] my address which was a memorial for Golda Meir. I do not write out addresses of this kind. I speak from rough notes, and I am sorry that the address was not taped, for I have received a number of requests for it. . . . I should tell you that The Course of Our Times is still making the rounds. In this area I think it comes in on Channel 44. Occasionally, also, some new programs come in on the Public Broadcasting System Channels where I am in dialogue with Hugh Downs on his show entitled "Over Easy." I am to do a new series with him for the year that begins in the fall. At the present time, I am underway on a new volume, an overview of the post-Holocaust years, "The Redemption Of The Unwanted." This will not be published, however, until the latter part of 1981. . . .

. . . Let me take the opportunity to congratulate you and Mrs. Yoken on the arrival of little David. If you are thinking of him for Brandeis, it is not too early to file an application for admission. This has become such a good school that applications should come in when the pregnancy test is positive! . . .

SCHULBERG, Budd, 1914-2009
American novelist and screenwriter. Dated 14 July 1970.

. . . At the moment, I am completing a screenplay based on the Puerto Rican migration to New York City, which I am doing with the Director, Elia Kazan, for whom I wrote and helped to produce "ON THE WATERFRONT" and "A FACE IN THE CROWD." We plan to shoot this film in Puerto Rico and Spanish Harlem at the end of the year. I have always been somewhat ambivalent in my writing interests since I like to work in the film medium as well as in fiction. And indeed, every so often, I am tempted to try the theater as well. I have never quite decided whether this versatility is a virtue or a defect.

I'm not sure if I have any direct literary influences. I was strongly affected by Scott Fitzgerald when I met him in his declining years, but of course his style is very different from mine. When I was in high school and college, I was fascinated with the Russian classics, with Dostoevsky as my favorite. In the '30s, I was impressed with the work of Frank Norris, who was in many ways a forerunner of Hemingway. My own rule was to write as simply and clearly, and honestly as I could, thinking about a clean presentation of the experience rather than about literary "style." I believe that the novel and the film have the dual purpose of entertaining and embodying strong social feeling. For this reason, I have admired the political novels of Silone, Malraux and Koestler.

After Kazan and I have completed our Puerto Rican film, I plan to devote myself to another novel with a Hollywood background, as Hollywood, strangely enough, was my home until I went off to college and its vicissitudes of fortune made a deep impression on me at a vulnerable age.

Another activity in which I continue to be involved is the support of the Watts Writers Workshop, an innovative ghetto school I founded after the holocaust in Los Angeles five years ago. Perhaps you have seen the Anthology I edited, "From The Ashes – Voices of Watts." The paperback edition is now being used in many black studies programs. . . .

SEXTON, Anne, 1928-1974
American poet. Dated 23 April 1969.

. . . My present activities involve working on a play and writing more poems, going to my psychiatrist and soon I'll be swimming. My favorite poet is Pablo Neruda who is a Chilean. Next to that Rainer Maria Rilke. . . .

Dated 21 April 1973.

. . . TRANSFORMATIONS sold very well and received almost entirely exciting and favorable reviews in the United States. In Britain it was despised. Why, I do not know. Maybe humor cannot cross an ocean, or maybe they felt I despoiled the Union Jack, although one would think it would be the Germans that would put up the fuss. . . .

. . . I do occasionally go out to universities across the country and give readings, but for a great deal of money, for, as you know, poets are not paid so much for their writing as for their reading in public. . . .

Dated 1 April 1974.

. . . I am so pleased that my poetry moves you, in fact moves you to translate it into French.

I am a totally primitive poet with no visible education, and although I hope I can write a good poem in English, I do not know French. But I do have friends who are fluent in French and will share your poem with them and treasure it for your love of the poem in any language. . . .

SHARP, U. S. Grant, 1906-2001

US Admiral. Dated 22 September 1971.

... Since I retired in July of 1968, I have been employed as a consultant to the President of Teledyne Ryan Aeronautical in San Diego. I am also Chairman of their Advisory Board. I have also been, at times, consultant to other companies in the aerospace business. I'm also active in some community affairs and have been involved in making speeches from time to time. I'll enclose copies of my two latest speeches to give you an idea of what my position has been on several matters that are important to our national security. ...

... I don't believe I can single out any particular influence [in my career]. I have tried to make the most of each assignment and give it the best I had. Putting out my best effort was made easy for me by a very understanding wife. We have had forty-one years of most pleasant married life. ...

... Quite naturally, the last four years of my career was the most notable, since during that period I was Commander in Chief Pacific. Perhaps the most satisfying particular element of that period was my success in getting the four military services in my area welded into a very smooth functioning team with a minimum of interservice conflict and a maximum of working for the most beneficial results for the nation. ...

SIKORSKY, Igor Ivanovich, 1889-1972
Inventor, aviation pioneer. Dated 10 March 1971.

. . . I consider as highlights of my career the design, construction and piloting of the first multiple-engined airplane in the world, in Russia during the year 1913 and the creation and development of the first practical helicopter in the western hemisphere in 1939.

However, the source of my greatest satisfaction lies in the great [number] of lives (by now several tens of thousands) which have been saved and continue to be saved by the helicopter. . . .

SINGER, Isaac Bashevis, 1903-1991

Writer, awarded Nobel Prize. Dated 13 January 1969.

. . . I have no writers of predilection. When I find a good book I enjoy it, no matter to what nation the writer belongs. However, I read very little fiction lately. As to the world situation, I am as blind and confused as anybody else. Naturally, I believe that if humanity could keep the Ten Commandments, ninety percent of our troubles would be gone. But the keeping of the Ten Commandments is not a simple matter. Some of them are almost against human nature. . . .

SONDHEIM, Stephen, 1930-2021
Composer. Dated 12 March 1992.

. . . Sorry to hear the lecturers and critics are still attacking me, but I suppose it's perpetual and inevitable. . . . I'm beginning to write two one-act musicals with James Lapine and have virtually finished a half-dozen songs for a musical movie, to be directed by Rob Reiner. And yes, I was indeed a Visiting Professor at Oxford two years ago. I enjoyed teaching, and had a very good time for the six months that I was (sporadically) there. . . .

STILL, Clyfford, 1904-1980
American painter, abstract expressionist. Dated 24 June 1971.

. . . After occasional glances at the published reports on the character, activities and work of one Clyfford Still, your comments offer a surprising and refreshing relief. By whatever course you have arrived at the attitudes suggested in your generous words, I must be pleased by the knowledge that the absurdities of irresponsible writers do not prejudice totally the minds of those like yourself. Such reassurance is always welcome. I must refer here to a coincidence that intrigues me. When my work was first generally made visible in the early 1940s, the first notes of appreciation came not from the American professionals in the critical field but from France and those of French extraction in the United States. The uncomprehending Greenbergs and Hesses appeared only after the work, by virtue of its influence on other artists, became politically and socially exploitable. Thus the situation became so offensive I chose to move away from what had become a commercial arena. . . .

. . . My time is spent in those activities that pertain directly to the continuation of my work. Fortunately, time and age have relieved me of many of those pressures of which younger men must take cognizance however wasteful or enervating they may be. . . .

. . . The purpose and development of my work precludes my indulgence in such a luxury [as deciding a best or favorite work]. I must save such pleasures for the lesser categories of value. . . .

. . . Insomuch as I have spent my life in the presence and study of works of art not only in painting but also in music, literature and philosophy, I recognized that my predilection and foci of analyses lay in the graphic media. Inevitably, my early years were spent in study and understanding of every available work of art, which came to my attention in the mastering of principles and means. By the age of twenty, I had literally "gone through" the ocean of "art," and by twenty-five or twenty-six years of age, I concluded that for me, the medium should have a far more significant role than that which I saw in past cultures or in the efforts of those of the present. In subject matter, means, method and purpose, I chose a different goal. In summary: those I had seen and studied revealed what had been done, and taught me *what not to do*.

I reread the above in some amazement that I have written at such length. But your cordial letter suggests a most civilized tolerance. I will have Mrs. Still type this, for my script is nearly illegible. I am sure you will forgive my gesture. . . .

TUCHMAN, Barbara, 1912-1989
Author. Undated, postmarked 1969.

. . . My favorite authors change from time to time (though I could mention Jane Austen, Chekhov, Anatole France). I am working presently on a biography of General Joseph Stilwell. My opinion on the current world situation is too dismal to discuss. . . .

Dated 3 October 1972.
. . . THE PROUD TOWER is my favorite [work] among my own –

The CHINA piece will be out in a small paperback about December 1st along with my current piece in FOREIGN AF-FAIRS (October) and a coming one in Harper's (December). I have just been reading proof today. . . .

WEST, Morris L., 1916-1999
Novelist and playwright. Dated 29 April 1971.

. . . Re the film version of "SHOES OF THE FISHERMAN." Let us say I would rather forget it. . . .

Dated 29 May 1991.

. . . A television mini-series has been made of CASSIDY, which has already appeared here in Australia. I have recently completed a new novel and am now working hard on another. So, if keeping busy is the secret to longevity, . . . many more birthdays to come should be granted! . . .

WHEELER, Burton K., 1882-1975
Senator from Montana, attorney. Dated 28 April 1970.

. . . After I got out of the Senate, I opened a law office with my son, Edward, here in Washington, D. C. under the firm name of Wheeler & Wheeler. I still get into my office every morning around ten a.m. and stay until around four in the afternoon, although I must confess I don't do very much work anymore. I play a little golf when the weather is good, and in January and February, I generally go out to Arizona for some golf and fishing.

The person who influenced me most to really take up the study of law was the principal of the Hudson High School, a Mr. Williams. When I was about to graduate he came to me and said that the teachers there had all been discussing what they thought the various students ought to do after graduation, and all of them agreed that I should study law. I told him I had always wanted to study law, but when my mother passed away a couple of years before, I had given up the idea of law, and that I gave up the study of French and Latin and took a business course in the high school in addition to my other studies, so consequently I would not be entitled to a regular diploma. A few days later, Mr. Williams came back to me and said that he found I had done more work than any other student in high school. He asked me if I would promise to go to law school if they gave me a regular diploma. I told him I would but that I would have to work a while to make some money as I had none and had no one to give me any or to lend me any. I worked a couple of years as a stenographer in Boston and Southbridge, Massachusetts for the American Optical Company and for the Draper Co. at Hopedale. I asked the Draper Company to give me $18 a week (I was getting $15) and they said they wouldn't do it unless I would stay there until January 1st, as I had been there only a few months. So I quit and went out to Michigan, waited table in the student's boarding house, and worked in the office of Dean Hutchins, who afterwards became President of the University of Michigan. Then on summer vacation I went out and sold books in Illinois. When I graduated Dean Hutchins wanted me to go to New York and said he would get me in one of the big law offices there. I told him I didn't want to go to New York but wanted to go west. He told me if I wanted to make any money, I would have to go where the money was, and he tried to discourage me, but I was determined to go west, and if you have read my book, "YANKEE FROM THE WEST" you will note that I went broke in Butte, Montana when I was about to leave and had to stay there.

The Anaconda Copper Co. had dominated the politics of Montana with an iron hand. They owned practically all of the daily newspapers; they controlled, through subsidiaries, nearly all of the county weekly newspapers; they completely dominated the economic life of the state with their mines and mills and banks, and they boasted that they never lost in a governorship race and that every senator that had ever been elected was their man. They beat Senator Thomas J. Walsh in 1910 for the Senate; he was elected in 1912 but only after somewhat of a compromise with the Company. In 1908 after I had been in Butte just a little over two years, they wanted me to go to the legislature. I turned them down. In 1910 again, they sent for me and asked me to go to the legislature, which I did. They made me chairman of the House Judiciary Committee and I was the youngest lawyer in the legislature. But I disagreed with them over the election of Walsh, whom they fought and defeated at that time, and then I disagreed with them on some other legislation. They offered me their money on different things, but in the senatorial fight a man whom I felt was their agent offered me $9,000! When I refused, he told me that I was the biggest damn fool of a politician that he ever knew, and I agreed with him! They told me I couldn't go back to Butte, but I said, "If I have to, I will leave with more money than I had when I got there." In 1912, they defeated me for Attorney General by a vote and a half and gave me only one of the fifty-nine votes of my home county, Silver Bow.

In 1913, Senator Walsh had me appointed US District Attorney. I had to prosecute the Democratic state treasurer, the Democratic state auditor, and I prosecuted one of the company's lawyers, a Democrat and former Attorney General, one of their closest friends, for tampering with the jury. I exposed Thiel, Pinkerton and Burns, detectives who were employed by the Company and who worked their way into the leadership, not only of the mineral union but also of the IWW's [Industrial Workers of the World]. In 1918, Walsh was coming up for election, and they told him they would beat him unless he got rid of me. At first he refused, but he finally told me that he was afraid they would beat him. I said, "If you feel that way, I will resign," and I did. Attorney General Gregory offered me a judgeship in Panama, which I turned down, telling him that I didn't need any job. I went back to Montana and the Non-Partisan League was just getting started. I scarcely knew the leaders but sent for them and told them I would help them organize. Through part of 1918, all of 1919 and part of 1920, I spoke all over the state and took up the issue of the Anaconda Company and their control of the legislature, the executive departments and the economic life of the state. In convention, the Non-Partisan League endorsed me for governor. They first wanted me to run on the Republican ticket, then they called and asked me to run on the Independent ticket. I turned them down, but finally they called and asked me to run on the Democratic ticket, which I did. Every newspaper in the state, with the possible exception of one or two, fought me bitterly. The billboards were covered with big red hands dripping with blood, and they threatened to close down all the mines and smelters and have the banks foreclose on the farm mortgages if I was elected, and said that we would have an economic catastrophe. I was the worst defeated candidate that ever ran for governor.

In 1922, the Non-Partisan League and labor groups wanted me to run for the Senate and I first told them no, but finally told them that if the League would not endorse me, I would run. I was opposed by the Speaker of the House, by a former Congressman and by the National Democratic State Chairman. I defeated all three of them by a few thousand votes and was elected to the Senate by, as I recall it, something like 18,000 votes. Two years later, in 1924, I ran for Vice President with La Follette.

I investigated Daugherty and he had me indicted both in Washington and in Montana. Forty-five years ago, I was acquitted by a jury in Montana, and the case in Washington was dismissed.

I became Chairman of the Senate Interstate and Foreign Commerce Committee in 1935 and handled some of Roosevelt's legislation, particularly one of his most important pieces of legislation, the Wheeler-Rayburn Utility Holding Company Bill. In 1937, I disagreed with Roosevelt on the Court Packing Bill and was given credit for defeating him on that issue. In 1939, he sent for me and asked me to handle the railroad legislation, and I handled it, after first telling him that I wouldn't do it. Only after he said that he would go along with me on anything I worked out did I agree to handle it for him, and it became known as the Transportation Act of 1940.

I afterwards disagreed with him on the war issue, and I was accused of being anti-Semitic pro-German and a Fascist, and money was sent in to Montana from New York, Chicago and Hollywood. They bought up labor leaders and farm leaders, and I was defeated in the primaries by a comparatively unknown man who had never done anything to amount to anything. I was afterwards defeated by a Republican.

I think probably my two greatest accomplishments were when I licked the Anaconda Copper Company and when I licked Roosevelt on the Court Packing Bill. . . .

WOLFE, Tom, 1930-2018
Author. Dated 5 September 1980.

. . . I'm not going to schedule any speaking engagements this fall due to a tour that my publishers have scheduled for me. I have a new book, IN OUR TIME, mostly drawings, that is coming out, as well as the paperback edition of THE RIGHT STUFF. I also have a long piece on architecture for the October issue of HARPER'S. It will expand on my remarks in BOOK DIGEST. As you can readily see, I am very busy. . . .

ACKNOWLEDGEMENTS

Many people have helped in variegated ways while I was preparing and organizing the contents of this longawaited book. I would like to acknowledge these individuals and the particular quality of each kindness that was shown me.

First, I would like to express my most sincere and profound thanks to Dr. John Twomey, Chancellor Professor Emeritus of Spanish Language and Literature at the University of Massachusetts Dartmouth, my dear and long-time friend and colleague, who has always encouraged me from the beginning stages of my work on this book. I owe him a very large debt of gratitude for his comments and support.

Next, I would like to express my deep gratitude to another long-time friend and colleague, Dr. Jean-Pierre Berwald, Professor Emeritus of Romance Languages at the University of Massachusetts Amherst. His astringent mind and friendly, steadfast interest in this work have proven to be an invaluable asset.

The late Dr. Vernon Ingraham, distinguished English

Professor at the University of Massachusetts Dartmouth, one of my best friends, guided me from the very outset of my opus. His cherished memory will forever be a guiding light, and I will always be grateful for his introduction and unending appreciation of my work.

The three aforementioned distinguished professors have always encouraged me in my life's work, and their sagacious counsel and generous hearts have helped me on my way to accomplishing many projects, literary and others, throughout more than five decades.

It is a pleasure to acknowledge my genuine indebtedness to both Elaine Brookfield and Katy Shoemaker for their sapient recommendations offered during the early stages of this book. Marion Dreyfus, too, has encouraged me from the beginning, and I would indeed be remiss if I failed to mention this affable, brilliant and literary lady who knows a great deal about literature and the publishing world. Next, my good friend Glen Chandler, whose wisdom and encouragement has sustained me through periods of unremitting support. My deepest thanks go out to Glen for his inspiration about my writing and his unflagging efforts to further the completion of this book.

I am beholden to Avery Hamlin, who has worked with me on this book over the past two years. Her suggestions, encouragement, and confidence have proven to be an inordinate help in the research and development of this work. I would also like to extend my thanks to Avery for designing the collage on this book's cover.

It takes a lot of editing to construct and assemble such a book. I relied on Morgan Beard to read and reread the quotes. Therefore, his astute and decisive preparation of the text for publication deserves special thanks.

I would like to thank most sincerely and wholeheartedly my beloved, incomparable family which includes my wife,

Cindy, my sons, David, Jonathan and Andrew, their wives, Dara and Jody, and my six grandsons, Ryder, Tommy, Mason, Weston, Jonah and Eli. They have helped me judiciously and patiently, and I can only hope that what I have done is worthy of their heartfelt faith, devotion and interest. There are none better and, succinctly, this book would not exist without them. Honestly, this book is a love letter, and it is addressed directly to my dearest family.

Last, but not at all least, to all the wonderful and celebrated individuals whose excerpts of letters I have included in this opus, I would like to say *merci de tout coeur.*

ABOUT ATMOSPHERE PRESS

Atmosphere Press is an independent, full-service publisher for excellent books in all genres and for all audiences. Learn more about what we do at atmospherepress.com.

We encourage you to check out some of Atmosphere's latest releases, which are available at Amazon.com and via order from your local bookstore:

The Great Unfixables, by Neil Taylor

Soused at the Manor House, by Brian Crawford

Portal or Hole: Meditations on Art, Religion, Race And The Pandemic, by Pamela M. Connell

A Walk Through the Wilderness, by Dan Conger

The House at 104: Memoir of a Childhood, by Anne Hegnauer

A Short History of Newton Hall, Chester, by Chris Fozzard

Serial Love: When Happily Ever After... Isn't, by Kathy Kay

Sit-Ins, Drive-Ins and Uncle Sam, by Bill Slawter

Black Water and Tulips, by Sara Mansfield Taber

Ghosted: Dating & Other Paramoural Experiences, by Jana Eisenstein

Walking with Fay: My Mother's Uncharted Path into Dementia, by Carolyn Testa

FLAWED HOUSES of FOUR SEASONS, by James Morris

Word for New Weddings, by David Glusker and Thom Blackstone

It's Really All about Collaboration and Creativity! A Textbook and Self-Study Guide for the Instrumental Music Ensemble Conductor, by John F. Colson

A Life of Obstructions, by Rob Penfield

Troubled Skies Over Quaker Hill: A Search for the Truth, by Lessie Auletti

ABOUT THE AUTHOR

Dr. Mel B. Yoken is Chancellor Professor Emeritus of French
Language and Literature at the University of Massachusetts
Dartmouth, where he began teaching French in 1966.
Though retired, he is very active in the university and its
surrounding communities.

Born and raised in Fall River, Massachusetts, Dr. Yoken
earned his Master of Arts in Teaching at Brown University,
and his Ph.D. in French Language & Literature from the Five
College Consortium.

He is the author of eight books and was recognized with
the French Legion of Honor.

Dr. Yoken lives in New Bedford, Massachusetts with his
wife Cindy. He has three sons, two daughters-in-law, six
grandsons, and countless friends.

CPSIA information can be obtained
at www.ICGtesting.com
Printed in the USA
BVHW050034051122
650904BV00002B/106